TRAPPED
in C@AVE!

TRAPPED in a CAVE!

A TRUE STORY BY
DEBORAH MORRIS

BROADMAN
& HOLMAN
PUBLISHERS

Nashville, Tennessee

4240-03

ISBN: 0-8054-4003-8

Dewey Decimal Classification: J796.5
Subject Heading: Caves
Library of Congress Card Catalog Number: 92-40731
Printed in the United States of America

Scripture quotation is from the Holy Bible, *New International Version*, copyright © 1973, 1978, 1984 by International Bible Society.

Library of Congress Cataloging-in-Publication Data

Morris, Deborah, 1956-
    Trapped in a cave! : a true story / Deborah Morris.
        p.   cm.
    ISBN 0-8054-4003-8
    1. Caving—West Virginia—Accidents—Juvenile literature.
I. Title.
GV200.655.W4M67   1993
796.5'25'09754—dc20   91-40731
                                                            CIP
                                                            AC

To Gary, Buddy and Tim Lutes, and also to the brave men and women of the National Cave Rescue Commission, real-life heroes who freely donate their time to help others.

CONTENTS

1

A Summer Adventure

I usually hate it when teachers assign those dumb "What I Did On My Summer Vacation" essays in school. But this year, starting eighth grade, I was almost disappointed when nobody asked about my summer. They'd never have believed what *I* ended up doing!

The whole thing started one weekend last February. My dad was cleaning our garage, and I was getting ready to ride bikes with James, my best friend. About that time my kid brother, Tim, showed up.

"What are you guys doing?" he asked as I wheeled my red BMX out of the garage. "Where are you going? Can I come?"

I ignored him, rolling my eyes at James, who grinned and shook his head in sympathy. James and I are a lot alike—both thirteen, blond, and kind of skinny—and he knew Tim always tried to follow me everywhere. He also knew I wanted to escape before my dad had a chance to decide I should help with the garage.

TRAPPED IN A CAVE!

We had almost made it to the sidewalk when Dad yelled, "Hey, Buddy, look at this!" Dad and Tim call me "Buddy" instead of my real name, Gary Lutes, Jr.

I turned around slowly, almost wishing I'd pretended not to hear. Dad was pulling a dusty cardboard box down from some shaky metal shelves.

"Here's all our caving gear from last year," he said. "I was just thinking, how would you and Tim like to go caving again this summer—maybe right after school lets out? I can probably take a week off from work around then."

Tim yelled, "All *right!*" and I grinned and said, "Sure!" That's one thing about my dad; he's always as ready for adventure as we are. Sometimes I think he likes having us around as an excuse to go out and play once in a while.

Dad is a land surveyor, a guy who helps other people figure out where to put bridges, highways, and things. He works a lot, but he spends as much time as he can with Tim and me—partly to have fun, but mostly, I think, because he worries about us not having a mom.

I guess I should explain right here about my mother. Her name was Linda, and she had dark blue eyes and long blond hair. I remember she was kind of pretty, and when Tim and I were little she used to take us for long walks. But Mom died of cancer when Tim was five and I was eight. Since then it's been just the three of us taking care of each other.

A SUMMER ADVENTURE

We order in pizza about once a week, take turns washing dishes, and sometimes play miniature golf on weekends. And every summer we try to find something exciting to do, like going camping or hiking, or even *spelunking*, which is a strange word for cave exploring.

Two summers ago we drove from our house in Tampa, Florida, to West Virginia, to a cave my dad had explored when he was a teenager. It was the first time Tim and I had been in a "wild" cave, with no lights or signs, and it was pretty creepy, cold, and dusty, and so tight in places that we had to crawl. There were weird markings on the walls, and I almost stepped on a huge brown rat with shiny red eyes. We had a great time, even though Dad kept reminding us not to "deface the cave's natural beauty." I guess he thought we might've brought along spray paint or crayons or something to create our own cave drawings.

Now, back home in our garage, Dad started pulling stuff out of the box and spreading it out on the concrete floor.

"My kneepads!" I said, grabbing the thick rubber cups with tangled elastic straps. I found my black hard hat and the little brass lamp that fits onto the front of it, like a miner's headlamp. I had used it for the first time the year before.

"I think this time we might try another cave in West Virginia," Dad said, "one called New Trout. It was named after a big rock that used to be there that looked like a fish jumping out of the water. Your mom and I went there once a long time ago, when we were first married. It was pretty safe."

When James and I finally took off on our bikes a few minutes later, Dad and Tim were still rummaging through the box, talking about exploring New Trout.

Looking back, it seems I should have *felt* something that day—a tingle of fear maybe, or at least a small shiver down my spine. But if there was any warning about what was going to happen, I was too excited to notice.

2

School's Out!

I usually like school—except for social studies—but it's hard to concentrate on books when you have a whole week of camping and caving to look forward to.

A few things happened, though, to liven up the wait.

First, there was the great student-teacher experiment. Nathan, a guy in my geography class, got to teach our class one day while Mr. Jackson, our *real* teacher, went and sat in the back. It was supposed to help us learn what it's like to be a teacher.

But when Nathan stood up at the beginning of class and said, "Please open your books and turn to page 43," everybody either laughed or ignored him. It made him really mad.

"Come on, you guys," he said, his face all red. "I'm the teacher!"

But the more he tried to tell us what to do, the harder we all laughed. Finally, Nathan got so mad he started shrieking at the top of his lungs:

"Listen to me! Listen to me!" It was so funny I thought I was going to choke.

That's when Nathan made his big mistake. Adam, another kid in my class, was mimicking him, saying, "Listen to me, students! I'm the *teeea-cher!*" Nathan stormed over and slapped his hand down on his desk.

"I've about had it with you, Adam!" he shouted. "You're just about the dumbest person in this whole school, you know that?"

Suddenly, the whole class got quiet. Adam stood up slowly, putting his face right up to Nathan's.

"What did you say?" he hissed.

Nathan swallowed hard, but he said it again. I guess they both forgot Mr. Jackson was still sitting in the back of the room, because a second later they lit into each other, hitting and kicking.

We all started yelling, "Help! Fight!" as Mr. Jackson jumped up and ran to the front.

He grabbed Nathan and Adam, pulling them apart. "You two know better than to act like this," he told them. "You can both march yourselves down to the office to see the principal."

"But, he wouldn't do what I said!" Nathan said, almost crying. "You said I was in charge!"

Mr. Jackson just looked at him. "Now you know how *I* feel some days when *you* act up." Nathan hung his head and shuffled off with Adam to the principal's office.

SCHOOL'S OUT!

The second thing that happened wasn't funny at all.

One morning around the middle of April, Dad woke up feeling sick and having trouble breathing. He looked all pale and sweaty and said his chest was aching. It kind of scared Tim and me. What would we do if something ever happened to Dad?

After a few days he got better, but then it happened again. Finally, when he got sick for the third time, my Aunt Jean came over.

"Gary Lutes, you get yourself to a doctor right this minute," she scolded him. Even though she's not much taller than me, Aunt Jean knows how to handle my dad, probably because she's married to his brother, Jim. "Will you go by yourself, or am I going to have to drag you there?"

Dad went, and a bunch of doctors ran tests on him. It turned out that his heart was "palpitating," beating irregularly, and that was why he was feeling so bad. The doctors said it wasn't too serious and gave him some pills to take. Tim and I were really relieved.

Finally, June rolled around and school ended. We started getting ready for our caving trip. Dad looked at maps to decide which campgrounds to stop at on the way, and we checked all our equipment. He said we could leave early Saturday morning, June sixteenth.

That Friday, I spent most of the day playing video games. Tim always teased me about playing so much, but he was just as bad. I'd been saving my money for months to buy a new game; in another week or two I figured I'd have enough.

"When you get that new game, are you going to let me play it?" Tim asked me that afternoon, trying to look innocent. He has big eyes and lots of freckles, and my dad usually falls for that look. But I know better.

"No way!" I told him. "I'm buying it with my own money, so you can just forget it." His face fell, and for a minute I almost felt bad. But he can be a real pain sometimes, and I wasn't in the mood to be nice.

You have to understand what it's like to have a little brother. They're always bugging you and getting into your stuff, and if you ever make the mistake of saying that you're about to do something—like watch TV, or play video games—they rush to get there first.

Even worse than that, though, is that half the time, *you* get blamed if they do something wrong.

"You're older, and I expect you to watch out for your little brother." "You're supposed to be a good *example!*" It's like God puts them in your family just to keep you from having fun.

I have to admit, though, that sometimes it's nice to have Tim around to do things with. Like on that Friday night, after Dad loaded all our camping and caving gear into the back of our Mazda truck, Tim and I went in the kitchen and started making sub sandwiches to put in our ice chest. We cut the rolls and squirted on the mustard, racing to see who could make them the fastest. Before we knew it, we had a dozen subs sitting on the counter.

Dad laughed when he walked in and saw the mountain of sandwiches.

"I guess you guys don't plan to starve on the road, huh?" he said. "Don't forget to pack some drinks."

Later on, Aunt Jean and Uncle Jim dropped by. "Well, are you boys excited about this trip?" Uncle Jim asked. He looks a lot like Dad—tall, with dark brown hair and a mustache. I grinned when he walked up and ruffled Tim's hair; people do that all the time.

Tim glared when he saw me smiling, so I smiled harder and mouthed the word *cute*. He looked like he was going to explode.

"You want me to keep an eye on the house while you're gone?" Uncle Jim asked. "I can stop by every day after work."

"I'd appreciate that," Dad said. "I'll leave the automatic garage door opener with you so you can get in."

Later we all sat down in the living room. Dad leaned back in his recliner and put his feet up, his hands behind his neck.

"We're planning to head up toward West Virginia first to do some camping and caving," he told Uncle Jim, "then next Thursday we'll go visit Linda's parents for a few days. They've been asking to see the boys for months."

"All right!" Tim interrupted. He was sitting on the floor, leaning against the coffee table. "Maybe Pop and Grandma will take us to Water Country USA again this year."

Our grandparents lived in a Texas-style ranch house near Richmond. Pop was a retired army colonel who talked with a thick Texas drawl; Grandma was short and plump with dark curly hair. They played rummy and Monopoly with us whenever we wanted, took us to amusement parks and video arcades, and let us explore the woods by their house. I always liked visiting them.

Dad and Uncle Jim were still talking. "Do you need to borrow any extra ropes or rappelling equipment this trip?" Jim asked. He'd been caving a few times, but I don't think he liked it as much as Dad.

Dad shook his head. "Nah, we're just doing some easy caves up around Franklin. I don't want to take the boys into a cave that requires any serious climbing. It's too dangerous for beginners."

Uncle Jim nodded, then yawned. "Well, I guess we'd better get out of here so you guys can get some sleep. What time are you leaving in the morning?"

"Before sunup. We're going to try to make it to the Carolinas by tomorrow night."

We all walked Uncle Jim and Aunt Jean out to

19
SCHOOL'S OUT!

their car. Aunt Jean hugged Dad, then Tim and me. "Have a good time," she said with a smile. "And you guys be careful, OK?"

Dad grinned. "Who, us?"

Aunt Jean rolled her eyes. "I mean it," she insisted. "Don't take any chances. I want all of you back safe and sound next week."

3

Saturday

When my alarm went off at 4 a.m. with a loud *beep-beep-beep,* I groaned and slapped at it to turn it off. At first I couldn't remember why I had set my alarm so early on a Saturday. Then it all came back to me—today we were leaving on vacation!

I jumped out of bed, suddenly wide awake, and ran into Tim's room. His alarm was beeping, but he had his head buried under his pillow. I jerked the pillow away and whacked him with it.

"Wake up, twerp. It's almost time to leave." I turned off his alarm. When he still didn't move, I shook his arm. "Come *on,* Tim. It's vacation, remember?"

He sat up then, rubbing his eyes like a little kid. I smiled and ruffled his hair, which was sticking straight up. "You know, you're not so bad when you're asleep," I told him affectionately.

"Cut it out," he mumbled. I guess he wasn't ready for compliments that early in the morning.

SATURDAY

Thirty minutes later we were ready to go. Dad checked that all the doors were locked and that we'd left the bathroom light on to scare off burglars—like burglars would steal the sink or something, right? Then we got into the truck, trying not to wake any of our neighbors.

It's always exciting to leave on a trip in the middle of the night when it's still pitch black outside and no one else is moving around. Instead of feeling sleepy I was wide awake, staring at all the dark houses we were passing. But Tim, sitting wedged between Dad and me, was drooping again, his head leaning against my shoulder. I guess I must've been weaker than I thought from lack of sleep, because instead of shoving him off I tried to hold still so I wouldn't wake him.

We drove for a couple of hours, not talking much. The sun came up, and we started seeing more cars on the highway. Finally, around 7 a.m., Tim sat up and looked around.

"Where are we?" he asked sleepily.

"Near Ocala," Dad told him. "What do you say we stop in a few minutes and have breakfast?" Tim and I both said, "Sure!" so at the next rest area, Dad pulled off.

We got out and stretched, then dragged the cooler out of the truck and put it on a picnic table surrounded by pine trees. We had packed a bunch of those little boxes of cereal—the kind you can open on one side and pour the milk right into the box—and we each got to pick one. I chose Frosted Flakes, and just to keep up my strength I ate some Cocoa Krispies, too. Tim ate some Froot Loops.

After we finished, Dad got out our football. "Let's get some exercise while we can. It's going to be a long day of driving."

Tim and I ran out for a couple of long passes and managed to catch the ball without slamming into any trees. I raced him back to the truck, then we loaded back up and headed north again.

We stopped for lunch around noon at the welcome center in South Carolina, then got right back on the road. By three o'clock my legs were starting to cramp, and I could tell Dad was tired, too. I was just wishing I was still young enough to whine, "Are we there yet?" when Tim turned to Dad.

"Are we there yet?" he whined. I burst out laughing, and Dad and Tim looked at me like I was crazy.

"Almost," Dad replied with his "we've-got-hours-more-to go-so-don't-start-complaining-now" look. I sighed and hunched down in my seat, trying to get comfortable.

Two hours later, we finally pulled into a campground for the night. We drove through the park slowly, looking for a spot to set up camp. By then I was so tired and hungry I would've gladly slept on an anthill, but Dad wasn't happy with any of the campsites.

SATURDAY

"They're all rocky and uneven," he complained. "Let's try somewhere else."

Just down the highway we found a "Yogi Bear" campground and pulled into a big slot with lots of trees. We unloaded our big cabin tent with a yellow roof and blue sides, then Tim and I set it up and shoved our cots and sleeping bags inside.

In the meantime Dad got out our camp stove, a little two-burner deal, and started cooking hamburgers and potatoes with string beans. I don't usually like string beans, but they smelled so good I was ready to eat them raw. I polished off about three burgers and two plates of potatoes before I even started feeling full.

After dinner, Tim and I went off into the woods with Dad's "Wrist Rocket" slingshot. It was still light outside, so we were hoping to spot a stray squirrel or bird or something to take a shot at. But Dad, probably on purpose, never let us practice much with his slingshot, so all we managed to hit were the trees.

"These small woodland creatures are sure safe with us," I told Tim in disgust as we started back toward camp. "We'd probably have better luck just sitting down and calling them."

We got back just as the sun was starting to go down. Dad had finished washing the dishes and was waiting for us.

"Why don't we walk over to the camp store and get some ice cream for dessert?" he suggested.

"There's a playground over there where we can sit and eat."

We bought three ice-cream bars, then went to the playground. There was a swing wide enough to hold all three of us, so we sat on it side by side, Dad in the middle. We started swinging, laughing at how silly we must look.

"You know what would be funny," Tim giggled, licking his ice-cream mustache. "What if somebody had a video camera out in the woods, and then they rigged this swing so it would break when people were on it. Like on 'Totally Hidden Video.' They'd be able to film all these people falling on top of each other."

"Let's hope that doesn't happen," Dad said. "We'd have ice cream smeared all over us."

I think God must have a really terrific sense of humor about some things, because just then the swing chain broke. Tim and I landed on top of Dad, the swing landed on top of us, and our ice cream landed *everywhere*. Mine was mashed into Dad's hair, Tim's was jammed in my right ear, and Dad's was halfway up Tim's nose.

We all yelled, "AAAAHHHH!"

It might have been better if someone had come out of the trees just then and said, "Ho-ho, you're on 'Totally Hidden Video!' Here's a check for $10,000!" But after we lay there for a while in the twilight and nothing happened, we finally got up.

"Well," Dad said weakly, wiping ice cream off his

SATURDAY

face. "I guess I've had about enough excitement for one day. Let's go clean up and turn in. We have another long drive coming up tomorrow."

We went to the bathrooms and washed up as best we could, then hiked back to our campsite. I drifted off to sleep listening to the bloodthirsty buzz of mosquitoes outside our tightly zipped tent.

4

Sunday

Waking up in a tent is always an interesting experience. Before you even open your eyes you know something is different, that you're not in your own bed at home. Your body starts sending a flood of exciting messages to your brain:

"I smell pine trees!" your nose shouts. "And bug spray! And wet canvas! Better get up!"

Then your ears chime in, "I hear strange birds singing and a fire crackling outside! Check it out!"

Almost before you know it, you're out of your sleeping bag and into your pants, stepping through a tent flap right into the great outdoors. There's nothing like it.

When we woke up Sunday morning it was foggy and humid, and not many campers were stirring around yet. Tim and I goofed around for a while, then around seven o'clock we "broke camp"—took down the tent and started loading our gear.

"We should be able to make it all the way to West

Virginia by tonight," Dad said, lifting the ice chest into the back of the truck. "Then first thing tomorrow morning we'll go explore New Trout Cave. That sound OK?"

"Sure!" I said happily. "I can't wait."

As we pulled up tent stakes and rolled our sleeping bags, we talked about our plans for the rest of the week. Going caving was going to be just the beginning.

"On Tuesday or Wednesday I'm going to take you guys to the small cliffs near where we'll be camping, and teach you some basic rappelling techniques," Dad said. Rappelling was using ropes to climb up and down steep surfaces; Dad was practically an expert. "Someday, after you both get good at it, I'd like to take you into one of the harder caves. New Trout is really just for practice."

We headed out, stopping for a quick breakfast at a rest area somewhere in North Carolina. We didn't break for lunch until we made it into West Virginia.

We were tossing the football around and talking about New Trout Cave when Dad suddenly slapped his forehead.

"You know what we forgot? We never bought any caving gloves! We'll need to stop somewhere; New Trout has a lot of broken rocks to crawl over, and I don't want you guys to tear up your hands."

We stopped at a grocery store just down the road and picked out three pairs of thick cotton gloves. We also bought more groceries to put in our cooler.

"These are the kind of gloves little old ladies use for gardening," Tim complained as we waited to check out. "They look stupid."

"So who's going to see them?" I asked. "The cave bats?" He stuck out his tongue at me, and for once Dad caught him.

"OK, guys, knock it off. We've only got a couple more hours to go, so try to act your ages." As usual, whenever Tim did something wrong I got yelled at too.

Around 3:30 p.m. we finally reached the campground where we planned to stay for most of the next week. It was near the south branch of the Potomac River, and we made sure to pick a campsite where we could hear the water.

"Isn't this great?" Dad said, looking around and sniffing the air. There were trees all around us, and the air was moist and cool and smelled of pine. "Let's get the tent up so we can check this place out."

We ate a quick dinner, then hiked through the woods toward the river. The water was clear and cold, bubbling over rocks and around small bends.

"Can we go wading?" I asked. "It looks pretty shallow."

"Sure," Dad said. "But first let's take off our shoes and socks and roll up our pants."

We all stepped into the water carefully, afraid that the smooth rocks would be slippery. But soon we were all splashing around, having water fights and collecting rocks off the bottom.

SUNDAY

"Hey, why don't we try to build a dam?" Da finally suggested. I guess he likes to help plan things, even on vacation. "We can pile some of these big rocks across that narrow bend in the river and see what happens. Maybe we can make a little waterfall."

We got busy dragging rocks and small boulders into a rough line. After awhile the water started surging up over the top of our rock dam, making little foaming rapids as it bubbled down the other side.

Finally, I sat down on the bank to rest. I tossed a few small pieces of wood into the water above our dam and watched them float faster and faster until they finally tumbled over the top of the rocks.

"Cool!" said Tim, plopping down on the grass beside me. "If we stacked enough rocks there, I bet we could stop the whole river!"

"I don't think we really need to do that, Tim," Dad said, rubbing his sore back. He had carried most of the big rocks.

We sat there for about an hour, just watching the water and talking. It was almost dusk before we finally returned to camp.

"You boys change into some dry clothes while I build a fire," Dad said. Tim and I ducked into the tent.

After we changed we went back out and plopped down next to the fire, which was still pretty small. We hadn't brought along very much wood.

TRAPPED IN A CAVE!

Dad glanced around hoping to find some dead branches we could use for firewood. You aren't allowed to cut down trees in a park.

But there were only small twigs lying on the ground. "Buddy," he finally said, "I want you to keep an eye on the fire for me while I scout around for more wood. Don't *play* with it; just *watch* it. OK?"

I rolled my eyes. "Sure, Dad." He acted like I might suddenly decide to start a forest fire or something just for fun. I guess he'd been watching too many Smoky the Bear commercials.

A few minutes later he came back, grinning, with a whole armful of logs. "I found these at an abandoned campsite. This should be enough to last the whole week!"

He took out our camp axe and started chopping the wood into smaller pieces, stacking them in a neat pile by the edge of our tent. I wanted to help, but he wouldn't let me.

"Maybe next year," he said. "I don't think I want you handling an axe quite yet." Great, now on top of him thinking I was a firebug, he figured I might hack my own leg off. You'd have thought I was six instead of thirteen.

Later that night, after we were all zipped into our sleeping bags, I was too excited to sleep, just thinking about our plans for the next day. Dad wanted to get an early start so we could be out of New Trout Cave in time for lunch; afterwards, we were going to go tubing down the river.

SUNDAY

"Dad?" I said in the darkness. "Can we roast some marshmallows tomorrow night after we get back?"

"Sure," he said. "And I'm planning to cook a big pot of that spaghetti you guys like so much for dinner. After a full day of caving and tubing, we'll probably be starved."

"Sounds good," I said sleepily. " 'Night, Dad. 'Night, Tim."

"Good night, Buddy," Dad said. Tim was already asleep.

5

Monday Morning

I woke up early the next morning ready to go, but Dad and Tim were still asleep. Dad was snoring, his mouth wide open, one corner of his mustache sticking down over his lip. One hand was hanging off the side of his cot, touching the floor.

I grinned, remembering the night at James's house when we put his sister's hand in a bowl of warm water while she was asleep, trying to make her wet the bed. I didn't think Dad would like that trick any better than James's sister did, or I would've tried it on him.

Instead, I crawled over to Tim's cot. "Tim!" I whispered, reaching over to jiggle his pillow.

As soon as I touched it, though, I jerked my hand back. "Oh, gross, Tim!" I yelled, wiping my hand on his blanket. "You drooled all over your pillow!"

Dad sat up and reached for his glasses. "What's all the yelling about?" he asked groggily. "What time is it?"

MONDAY MORNING

"Almost seven," I said, peering down at my digital watch. Actually it was 6:24, but I figured by the time he woke up enough to notice, it *would* be almost seven.

Sure enough, he just shook his head and reached for the overalls he'd tossed beside the cot the night before.

"We might as well get up and grab some breakfast, then. It won't hurt to get an early start. It'll take us about an hour to get to New Trout Cave."

He buttoned on a long-sleeve red shirt and stood up, hooking his overall straps over his shoulders. He looked kind of funny; I'd only seen him wear overalls a couple times before.

He saw me staring at him and grinned. "Both you guys need to dress warm, too. Caves get pretty chilly."

I pulled out my brown corduroy jeans and a blue-checkered flannel shirt, then started digging around under my cot for some clean socks. Since Tim still wasn't moving, I nudged him with my foot. He finally groaned and sat up.

"Food," I announced, keeping it simple. "Get dressed." Then I laced up my tennis shoes and followed Dad outside.

He was getting a carton of milk out of the cooler. "Let's just have some cold cereal and orange juice," he said. "I'd rather not build a fire since we're going to leave."

We planned to spend the next three nights at the

same campsite, so this time we didn't have to pack up everything. After breakfast we just loaded the cooler into the truck, zipped up the tent, and took off.

I stared out the passenger window for a long time, watching the trees flash by. For some reason I suddenly found myself thinking about Mom.

"Dad?" I said. "Didn't you and Mom first meet somewhere around here?"

Dad smiled. He always liked talking about his younger days, and I could tell he'd been thinking about things as we drove along.

"Sort of," he said. "I met her at my grandmother's house in Fairfax, a couple hours from here. My brother Jim and I went down to go fishing in Grandma's pond one afternoon, and your mom showed up there with a friend. She was eighteen and pretty good-looking, so I invited her over the next day to look at some slides Jim and I had taken of Cave Mountain Cave last time we'd been there. She pretended to be real interested."

I grinned at Tim, but he wasn't even listening. He still acted like talking about girls and stuff made him sick.

Dad was still remembering: "That summer, when your mom came home again from college, we started dating off and on. She wasn't like a lot of other girls, all prissy and afraid to get dirty. She'd go hiking and fishing with me and had as good a time as I did. She wasn't afraid to bait her own hook, either, with worms and shrimp. I thought she was great."

He laughed, his eyes wrinkling behind his glasses. "I don't know which of us was more surprised when I finally asked her to marry me. It just kind of slipped out one day when I was over at her house. I went home thinking, *Did I really say that?* But it turned out to be a great idea."

We rode along for a minute without talking, all of us suddenly feeling a little sad. Even after four years, I still missed Mom sometimes. I couldn't ever admit it to Dad, but whenever I spent the night at James' house I really enjoyed the way his mother fussed over me. Even their house was kind of different, fixed up with flowers and pictures and things. I mean, I had a Robocop poster on my wall, and Dad bought a fancy clock for the living room, but it wasn't the same. You could tell just guys lived at our house.

But even though I missed Mom, I had a hard time now remembering exactly what she looked like. It made me feel bad sometimes to think I could forget my own mother like that.

Dad was slowing down. "You guys need to start helping me watch for the trail up to New Trout," he said, peering over the steering wheel at the wooded mountainside to our right. "I think we're getting close."

I pasted my face to the passenger window, shoving Tim off my shoulder as he crowded over to look.

TRAPPED IN A CAVE!

A few minutes later I spotted a small dirt path leading up the slope.

"There it is!" I shouted. My voice came out in a squeak, so I cleared my throat and said again, "There it is, Dad." This time it came out better.

I turned around to glare at Tim, who was snickering the way he always did when my voice cracked. "Dad, will you make him *stop?*"

"That's enough, Tim. You're going to be in the same boat in a couple years, and you won't want people laughing at you."

Tim just rolled his eyes and kept grinning, so I "accidentally" elbowed him in the side. He squalled, "Dad!" but Dad just ignored him. I guess he figured Tim had it coming.

We pulled off the road onto the shoulder and got out. Dad stretched, and his bones made all these loud popping sounds.

"Getting old," he mumbled, swinging his arms back and forth to loosen up. When I said agreeably, "Yep, you sure are!" he laughed and took a swat at me.

All our caving gear was in the back of the truck, so we started pulling it out. I bundled up my hard hat, lantern and kneepads, and started up the steep slope. We left our lunches in the cooler since we planned to be out in plenty of time for lunch. It was only nine o'clock in the morning.

There were actually three separate caves at the top of the hill: Trout, New Trout, and Hamilton.

Hamilton Cave was the one we'd explored the year before, where we'd seen the big rat.

"Hey, here's the visitor's shelter!" I called down over my shoulder to Dad and Tim. Just outside the caves was a small wooden lean-to with pamphlets about bats and things, mostly telling people not to hurt them. There was also a notebook where visitors were supposed to sign in before they went into any of the caves.

Dad walked up and dropped his gear in a pile on the ground. "You guys go put on your pads and helmets while I sign in," he said.

New Trout Cave had a little wooden sign nailed up just above its entrance that said "New Trout" and had the National Speleological Society symbol, a half-circle with "NSS" in the middle. I sat down underneath it to pull on my kneepads, making sure they were tight. I'd found out last time that if they were too loose they'd scoot right off my legs when I started crawling.

Tim was doing the same thing. Finally, Dad came over and sat down with us. "Hand me your headlamps," he said. "I'll go ahead and get them started for you."

He took my lamp first and unscrewed the bottom, dumping in some carbide granules from the can we'd used the year before. Then he screwed it back together and filled the top with a little water from our drinking bottle. When he turned a valve, the water started dripping down into the carbide, which formed a gas that could burn. When he flipped the small flint wheel it made a spark, and a blue flame appeared.

"Here you go," he said, handing it back to me. I hooked it onto the front of my plastic hard hat, then pulled the strap tight under my chin. While Dad was fueling the other two lamps, I got out my new gloves and wriggled my fingers into them. They were pretty stiff and scratchy, but I didn't care. I just wanted to get moving.

Finally Dad stood up. "OK, let's do it!" he said, ducking his head as he led the way into the cave.

When we first stepped inside, it wasn't all that dark, just kind of gloomy.

"You are now entering... The... Twilight... Zone," Dad joked as he moved deeper into the cave. For the first few feet, Tim and I could stand up straight, but soon the ceiling got so low that we had to duck, too. By the time we went around the first curve in the main tunnel, it was totally black. Our little headlamps suddenly seemed much brighter.

"Watch your heads," Dad told us. "These stalactites are hard to see in the dark."

I walked along just behind Dad, being careful about where I put my feet. There were lots of loose rocks that shifted when you stepped on them, and some tall, pointed stalagmites sticking up along the edges of the cave. I could almost picture tomorrow's headlines: "Boy Trips, Gets Stuck On Stalagmite Like Bug On Pin." No, thank you!

MONDAY MORNING

"Hey, look at this," Dad said, interrupting my imaginary demise. He was pointing to one of the cave walls just ahead.

I moved closer so my headlamp would shine directly on the wall. It was strange looking, black and shiny, with little popcorn-like lumps sticking out everywhere.

"Neat!" I said, touching one of the black popcorns with my gloved finger. "What *are* these things?"

"I'm not really sure what they're made of, but that's a formation called cave coral. If you keep your eyes open, you'll probably see all kinds of strange things in here today."

A little farther along we stopped to look at a brown bat hanging upside down, asleep, on the wall. It looked kind of cute, with soft brown fur and little pointed ears, but Dad wouldn't let us touch it.

"Bats are so sensitive that even your body heat can disturb them if you get too close," he said. "And if you startle them awake, they sometimes get so confused that they drop onto the floor and break their necks. They're very delicate."

We tiptoed away, leaving the little bat snoozing peacefully. Then Dad started telling us how New Trout and the other two caves had once been used as mines during the Civil War.

"With the saltpeter they took out of these three caves, they made over twenty-five thousand pounds of gunpowder," he said. "Some of the big sticks the workers used for torches are still lying around in here. You might find one if you watch for it."

He also said different people had found bones from extinct animals in the cave—ground sloths, dire wolves, even a saber-toothed cat!

"That's the exciting thing about caving," he said. "You can turn a corner or crawl through a hole, and suddenly be standing someplace no living person has ever been. There's just no telling what you'll find."

Tim giggled. "Like in 'Star Trek,' we're 'boldly going where no man has gone before!'" He cupped his hands around his mouth and said in a hollow voice: "Beam me up, Scotty! There's no intelligent life in here."

"Yeah, especially with *you* around," I sneered.

"Don't start anything, Buddy," Dad warned. "Let's keep going."

Each time we turned a corner, Dad stopped for a minute to study the tunnel behind us. "You have to pick out landmarks—rocks that are funny shaped, sticks lying a certain way—so you can find your way back out later." He motioned toward a cave wall where several chalk arrows were scrawled, each pointing in a different direction. "That's an amateur's trick, and a good way to get lost. Not to mention that it messes up the cave."

On our caving trip the year before, Dad had

made us memorize the NSS motto: "Take nothing but pictures. Leave nothing but footprints. Kill nothing but time." He had even brought along a plastic bag in his backpack in case we had to go to the bathroom. Tim and I both decided we'd rather wait till we got back out.

By now we were pretty deep in the cave. The air was chilly, and we could see our breath in the headlamps. I looked back at Tim and laughed; his nose was black, smeared with sticky cave dust. He looked like some kind of big, goofy dog.

"Your face is black, too," he retorted when I told him. "There's a big streak right down your cheek." I rubbed my face to get it off, but when I looked down at my gloves I saw they were both black, too. Now my whole face was probably dirty.

"Oh, great," I said. Tim just laughed.

Dad looked at us and grinned, his face also streaked with black. "'You guys know what this black stuff is, don't you?"

"No, what?" I asked.

"Ever hear of bat guano?"

"Oh, gross, Dad!" I said in disgust, turning to explain to Tim, "That means *bat poop!* But it isn't really. Is it, Dad?"

He laughed. "Nah, it's just manganese dioxide dust, left over from all the saltpeter mining. Then again, you never know; it might have a *little* guano mixed in with it. Maybe that's why it's so greasy."

"Oh, Dad," Tim said. "Give it up!"

"Yeah, parents aren't supposed to say gross stuff like that," I agreed.

We were still kidding around a minute later when we came around a corner into a large, open area. Huge boulders were leaning at crazy angles all around us, and several small tunnels led off in different directions. Dad glanced around quickly.

"I think this is the place called the Big Room. Let's take a break here so I can refuel all the lamps before we go on into the Maze."

"The Maze?" Tim asked.

Dad nodded, pointing to a low tunnel off to one side of the room. "There's a whole long series of passages in there that twist around each other, like a honeycomb or a maze. Most of it is so low you have to crawl. You guys want to have a snack now, while you can still move around? I brought along some trail mix and stuff in my pack."

"Sure," I said, picking a boulder to sit on. Even through my thick pants, the rock felt cold. "What do you have besides trail mix?"

"Well, let's see," Dad said, rummaging in his red pack. "Here's your water bottle, Buddy, and here," he pulled out a squished plastic bag, "are some petrified Gummi Bears, from that big bag Aunt Jean gave you guys awhile back. I think that's about it."

"I'll take the Gummi Bears!" Tim said, snatching the bag. "I don't care if they're old. I still like 'em."

Dad and I each scooped up a handful of trail mix

and sat back for a few minutes, chewing. It was funny how quiet the cave got once we stopped moving around. I could hear Tim gnawing at his Gummi Bears and Dad crunching the trail mix, and for a second I pictured the three of us as prehistoric cavemen, huddled over a meal of roast saber-toothed cat—Tim gnawing a leg, Dad nibbling a crispy paw.

Crunch, crunch. Gnaw, gnaw.

Suddenly, I lost my appetite. I quickly swallowed the trail mix, no longer sorry that all those saber-toothed cats and ground sloths that once prowled New Trout were extinct. I didn't think I'd want to face one on the dinner table that night.

Dad fueled each of our headlamps again, dumping the spent carbide granules into a small plastic bag. "Used carbide is poisonous," he explained as he stuck that bag into another bigger one to make sure nothing leaked out. "It could kill some of the animals in here if we weren't careful with it."

I took a swig from my water bottle and offered Dad some; he hadn't brought his own bottle this trip. He took a sip, then shoved everything back into his pack.

"Tim, why don't you lead off this time," he suggested, waving toward the Maze opening. "Buddy, you go next, then I'll bring up the rear. We'll have to go single file in these passages—they're really tight."

Tim dropped to his knees and crawled into the

first tunnel. I went in right behind him. "Watch yourselves," Dad cautioned. His voice sounded far-away, even though he was just behind me. "Make sure you can see where you're putting your hands and feet."

What none of us knew, as we slowly worked our way into the tight, twisting passages, was that we had missed something important back in the Big Room. Over in one corner, lying on a big, flat boulder, was another visitor's book we were supposed to sign before we entered the Maze. The book was sealed in a white plastic case labeled "New Trout." It was there to keep track of who'd gone deeper into the cave—and who'd come back out.

This time, however, we left behind "nothing but footprints"—no clue to show that we'd ever even been there.

6

The
Maze

Once we started into the Maze, the thick rock of the tunnel muffled our voices, making it hard to talk. I crawled along silently, kind of enjoying the sensation. It was almost like being alone in the cave, exploring all by myself. My breath came out in puffs of white smoke like dragon's breath. I felt like some powerful, scaly monster crawling along deep in its lair.

I was having a good time until I suddenly banged my head, hard, on a thick stalactite. "Yow!" I shouted, my voice sounding small. Even through my hard hat it hurt my forehead.

For a while the tunnel got a little wider. Then we reached a spot where a bunch of loose rocks had slid down, partially blocking our way. They half filled the passage we were in, sloping off into the darkness of an open area below. The only way to keep going was to crawl right across the rocks.

I went first, holding on with my hands and feet like Spiderman on a wall. A couple of times the rocks under my feet started wobbling, but I always managed to hang on. My heart was pounding as hard as if I'd been scaling a cliff instead of a little rock slide.

Finally, I reached the other side. When I turned around Tim was right behind me, grinning.

"You scared?" he asked. "That wasn't any big deal."

"Lay off, bat breath. I'm heavier than you are, so it's easier for me to slide."

"R-right. That's why you went so slow."

By then Dad was behind us, so we both shut up. "Let's go, guys. Take the tunnel to the left this time." He paused again to note some landmarks to mark our way out.

We walked and crawled through a few more passages before coming to a steep drop off. To keep going we'd have to climb down about eight feet, then squeeze through a narrow crack to get into the next tunnel. Dad hesitated, trying to decide whether we should go on or turn back.

"What do you think?" he asked, turning to Tim and me. "You feel like heading back now?"

It would've been fine with me. I didn't much like the idea of squeezing into another dark, tight tunnel. But after Tim had just bugged me about being scared on the rock slide, I didn't want to say anything.

Tim said, "Let's keep going!"

Dad nodded. "I guess we'll have to leave the

THE MAZE

backpack here," he said, eying the narrow squeeze just ahead. "We won't go much farther, just enough to see if it's worth the effort. It's never a good idea to get too far from your emergency supplies."

Our "emergency supplies," aside from the snacks and water bottles, were some candles and matches, the can of carbide fuel, an extra carbide lamp, and a flashlight. We were following another caving rule: You were never supposed to go into a cave without at least two backup sources of light, in case something went wrong with your lanterns.

"Caving is a lot like diving," Dad told us once. "Underwater, you need an airline to survive; under-ground, light is what keeps you alive. It's your only link back to the surface." Before we left home we had checked that our matches worked and put fresh batteries in the flashlight. Dad didn't like to take chances.

Now, since we were only planning to scout around for a few minutes, we shoved the red backpack to one side of the large rock ledge where we'd stopped. Dad checked the time, then set his stopwatch.

"We should have at least a half an hour of fuel left, but to play it safe we'll make sure to be back here in twenty minutes. Then we can decide if we've done enough exploring for the day." He motioned for Tim to lead off down the drop off and into the next tunnel.

TRAPPED IN A CAVE!

Even though I'm pretty skinny, getting through that narrow crack wasn't easy. I put my head through first, then kind of wriggled and squirmed until I got my legs and feet through. It was going to be fun to watch Dad try to make it through that little space.

Sure enough, it took him a few minutes. First, one of his overall straps got snagged; then his hips got stuck. Finally, he made it through and we kept going.

In one passage we found what looked like an old miners' torch, a thick stick with one end black and charred. I shuddered, thinking of crawling in the tight tunnel with a flickering torch and black smoke burning my eyes. I was glad we had our little carbide lamps.

It was right as I was thinking that, that Tim's headlamp suddenly flickered and dimmed. He half turned to face Dad and me.

"Hey, Dad? Why's my lamp doing this?"

We were all bunched up, so close that I could see Tim's dirt-smeared freckles. Dad glanced at his watch and frowned.

"I don't know, Tim; there should still be plenty of fuel left. But let's not take any chances. If the lamps are going to malfunction, we'd better get back to the pack."

Dad took over the lead, with Tim following, and me bringing up the rear. Tim's lamp was flickering so badly he could hardly see where he was going, so

THE MAZE

I kept shining my light ahead for him. Before long his lamp completely died.

We went a little farther, slowly because of Tim. Then *my* lamp suddenly sputtered.

"Hey!" I yelled, startled. With Tim's lamp out and Dad's headlamp pointed ahead, it had gotten very dark for a second.

Dad stopped and looked back, his light casting shadows all around us.

"OK, guys, we've really got to *move*," he said sharply. "I don't know what's happening, but we sure don't want to get stuck back in here. We need to get back to our pack."

His voice sounded kind of funny, like he was mad or something. Tim and I just said, "OK," and started forward again.

We moved as fast as we could, not even caring where we put our feet as we scrambled through the narrow tunnels in the flickering light. After another minute or so my lamp went out, too.

From then on, Dad had to keep turning his headlamp back and forth so Tim and I could see where we were going. We kept banging our heads and twisting our ankles in the dark tunnel. "I don't like this," Tim complained.

By then we should have been almost back to our supply pack. But, suddenly, Dad stopped.

Puzzled, I looked ahead to where his lamp was pointing. There was a long, twisted stick, propped sideways against the wall of the tunnel—something I didn't remember seeing on our way in.

I felt my mouth go dry. We were off our original path!

Before I could say anything, though, Dad said quietly: "Hey, guys, I think we need to turn around and backtrack for a minute. Let me get in front of you again."

"Are we lost, Dad?" I asked, not even caring that my voice came out in a squeak.

"No, it's just that I don't recognize this area," he said.

Tim and I looked at each other, both feeling a little scared. Dad had been caving for over twenty years, and he'd never lost his way before. Why did it have to be now, when our lamps were messed up?

We tried one tunnel that looked good, but after crawling for over a minute we came out again next to the same long stick. Then we tried a different, longer passage.

Even though the cave was cold, Dad's shirt was wet with sweat as we hurried along. When he stopped again, I knew something was wrong.

I looked past him, my stomach sinking when I saw what was outlined in his headlamp. It was the same long, twisted stick!

It was at that very moment that Dad's lamp, our *last* lamp, suddenly flickered and dimmed.

7

A Nightmare Comes True

Dad turned around slowly, his face hidden in shadow. "I think we're in trouble, guys," he said. This time he didn't sound mad, he sounded *scared*.

My heart started thudding against my ribs. "Dad, I want to get out of here," I said. "Can't we do something?"

He rubbed his forehead, trying to think. "Buddy, why don't you and Tim sit here together for a minute while I try to find the right path. I can move faster alone. Just keep shouting so I can stay within calling distance."

Tim and I sat down, our backs against a rock, as Dad turned and started back the way we'd come. I watched as his dim, flickering light bounced along the cave walls, moving away from us. When he finally stepped out of sight around a corner, Tim and I were suddenly left in total darkness.

"Hey, Dad!" I called, forcing my voice to be steady. "Can you hear me?"

His answer came back, sounding faint and far away. "Yeah. Just keep calling!"

Beside me in the dark, I could hear Tim sniffling, starting to cry. "Come on, you yell too," I told him. I didn't like sitting in the dark any better than he did, but it wouldn't help to bawl. "*Do* it, Tim!" I commanded.

"Dad!" he finally called, his voice all shaky. "Right here, Tim," Dad called back. His voice sounded nearer this time, and a moment later we saw his headlamp reflected against some rocks. Pretty soon he made his way back to where we were sitting.

"I didn't find it in that direction. I'm going to try again."

He started off in a different direction this time, and Tim and I started yelling again. When Dad finally came back, his light was pretty dim.

"This isn't going to work," he said. "My lamp is almost gone, and I don't want to take a chance on getting separated from you two. Let's all stay together from here on."

I didn't say anything, but I was relieved. Somehow, just being together made it seem not so bad.

We started off again, this time not rushing as much. Dad examined each turnoff carefully, hoping to find a familiar landmark. All the time his lamp kept sputtering, growing dimmer and dimmer.

We had just started into a low, cramped tunnel

with a deep pit to one side when Dad's headlamp flickered and died. Suddenly, we were plunged into total darkness.

For a second nobody moved or said anything. I was standing bent over, the back of my hard hat touching the low ceiling of the tunnel. I slowly lowered myself to a sitting position, feeling all around me like a blind person.

Finally Dad cleared his throat. "You guys OK?" he asked. "Yeah," Tim and I both answered.

"Listen, that pit is somewhere over here by me, so don't move. I'm going to try to get between you and it."

I could hear Dad moving around somewhere to my left, and Tim starting to sniffle again just behind me. I felt kind of numb, still not really able to believe what was happening. It was like one of those nightmares where you *know* it's a nightmare, so you think: *No big deal, I'll wake up in a minute and everything will be fine.*

Only this time, I knew it was real.

"What are we going to do, Dad?" I asked quietly. "Can we just keep crawling? Maybe hold onto each other's legs so we can stay together?"

He thought for a moment. "I don't think that would work, Buddy. There'd be too big a chance of falling and hurting ourselves. And if we couldn't find the right path with a light, there's not much chance that we'd stumble on it by accident. I think our best bet will be to just sit tight and wait for rescuers to show up."

"How will they know we're here?" I asked.

He thought about that. "Well, after a few days somebody will be sure to notice our truck sitting out by the highway, and they'll call the police. Then they'll send in trained cavers to find us."

I thought about having to spend several days in the dark, cold cave. It felt strange to have my eyes wide open but not to be able to see *anything*, not even a vague outline. I held my hand up in front of my face until it actually touched my nose, but it made no difference.

This must be what it's like to be blind, I thought.

Tim started sobbing, his breath coming in quick gasps. Dad tried to calm him. "We'll be all right, son. I'm just sorry I got you boys into this. It was a stupid move to leave our emergency pack like that. I should've known better."

"Do we have any water?" Tim asked tearfully. "Or food?"

I'd forgotten about that, but of course our snacks and water bottles were in the backpack with everything else. "I'm afraid not," Dad said heavily. After that there didn't seem much else to say.

I was considering what he'd said about some-body noticing our truck when a thought suddenly struck me. "Dad?" I said, thinking aloud. "What if somebody *steals* our truck? Does anybody else know we're here?"

The minute I said it I wished I could take it back, but it was too late. Tim started crying again, and Dad didn't say anything right away. We all knew the answer.

Nobody, not even Uncle Jim, knew exactly where we were.

8

Monday Afternoon

For a long time we sat without speaking. After about an hour my stomach started rumbling, sounding loud in the darkness. *Must be lunchtime,* I thought gloomily. I automatically glanced down toward my watch and remembered, suddenly, that it was the kind that had a small light built into it.

"Hey!" I said aloud, feeling for the knob. "Maybe our watches can give us enough light to get out of here! Try your lights and let's see!"

All three of us had the same kind of watches. I pushed the knob on mine and stared down at the dim green dot of light on my wrist, relieved to discover my eyes still worked. I looked over toward Tim, spotting another speck of light.

"Can you see me?" I asked, holding my watch up so it pointed toward my face.

"No," Tim said. "All I can see is your watch."

"Let's try putting them all together," Dad suggested. "Maybe that'll make them brighter."

MONDAY AFTERNOON

Carefully, we crawled toward each other, feeling our way over the rocks. But even when we held all three of our watches together, they still didn't give off enough light to see anything.

"Oh, well," I said, disappointed. "It was worth a try."

Pretty soon Dad's and Tim's stomachs started growling, too. "Boy, I sure wish we had those sub sandwiches out in the truck," Tim complained. "Or at least the gummi bears and water."

I poked him to make him shut up. Dad already felt bad enough. "We had a snack just before we came in here," I reminded him. "Get your brain off your stomach."

Dad wasn't saying much, but he must've been thinking. "I have an idea," he said after a minute. "Let's sift through the carbide in all our lamps, and try to pick out any unused pieces. Maybe we can get a lamp going again long enough to find a safer place."

Carbide fuel looks just like gravel until it's used, when it becomes fine, like sand. We carefully unscrewed the bottoms of our lanterns and started feeling through the spent fuel.

I pinched up a small amount and rubbed it between my fingers, letting it slowly sift back down into the lamp. On the third pinch I felt a small, hard piece, and kept it in my hand. I ended up finding three unused chunks.

Dad and Tim had each found a few pieces, too.

Putting them together we had about a teaspoonful. Dad emptied the used carbide from his lamp down into the rocks before placing the few good pieces back into the lamp.

"Where are you going to get water for it, Dad?" I asked, suddenly remembering that it took both fuel and water for the lamp to light. I didn't think spit would work.

"Well," Dad said, sounding embarrassed, "I'm probably going to go to the bathroom in it. We don't have many choices in here."

Tim giggled, and I grinned into the dark. "Way to go, Dad," I said.

A few minutes later he had the lamp ready to light. "OK, guys, as soon as I get it going, we need to move fast. We'll only have a minute or two at most."

He flicked the lamp's flint wheel, and a small blue spark flared and caught. I blinked, almost blinded by the sudden light. "Let's go!" Dad shouted.

We hurried through several short tunnels, looking for a better place to wait for rescue. Finally we found a large room with a huge, table-sized boulder.

"This will work," Dad said, seeing that there were no pits or other obvious dangers. "Quick let's all get up on that flat boulder before the lamp goes out again."

We scrambled up and sat side by side, Dad in the middle. "Take off your knee pads and sit on them," he told Tim and me. "It'll help insulate you from the cold rock."

I did what he said, shoving the thick rubber cups under me. They were lumpy and uncomfortable, but they did feel a little warmer than the boulder.

Dad's lamp was flickering weakly, the small blue flame now all but gone. I stared hard at it, as if by concentrating I could somehow make it stay lit. But a moment later it went out—this time, I knew, for good.

The darkness almost seemed worse now, after having had light again for a minute. I hugged my legs to my chest and leaned my head forward on my knees, suddenly feeling the cold.

Tim sighed. "Dad, when do you think somebody'll come find us?"

"It's hard to say, son. Tomorrow, maybe, or Wednesday at the latest. By then they'll definitely notice that our truck hasn't moved."

Two days without food or water. The idea kind of hung there for a minute, all of us thinking about it but not really wanting to say anything. No matter how you looked at it, it was terrible.

I must have dozed off just about then, because the next thing I knew my watch said it as 6 p.m. I yawned and stretched, bumping Dad with my right elbow. He had an arm around my shoulders, helping hold me up.

TRAPPED IN A CAVE!

"Have a nice nap?" he asked. "You were really snoring."

"Yeah," I replied. It was hard to wake up in the dark like that; it left me feeling all confused. I could hear Tim stirring around on the other side of Dad. I guess he must have fallen asleep, too.

Dad gave us a few minutes, then said: "Listen up guys, we need to talk about something. Now, while we're still pretty fresh, we should make some plans about how we're going to cope with several problems that might come up.

"The two biggest dangers are dehydration—the loss of body fluids—and hypothermia, the loss of body heat. So I want you to stay as still as possible; the less you move around, the less you'll sweat. And no matter how tired you get, *don't stretch out on the rock*. It's cold, and you'll just be speeding up the process of chilling your body."

I nodded my head, then caught myself and said aloud, "OK, Dad." But I was suddenly remembering how sweaty Dad's shirt had been earlier, and how he'd only taken one small sip of water before we started into the Maze. I could feel him shivering beside me, his shirt still slightly damp.

I wanted to say something about it, ask him what *he* was going to do to stay warm. But then I realized I was acting like a little kid, expecting him to have all the answers.

He was in just as much trouble as we were—and probably more.

*Left to right: Buddy, Gary
and Timmy Lutes*

*Marty Hardy at mouth
of New Trout Cave.*

Marty Hardy in room where
the Lutes were found.

The Lutes' rescuers, John Hempel and Marty Hardy, with the author.

9

Tuesday

I dozed off again, still sitting with my knees to my chest. It was almost 9 p.m. when a strange, rustling noise just above my head startled me awake.

I was still groggily trying to figure out what the sound was when suddenly, the air all around me exploded with the flutter of wings.

"Bats!" Dad shouted.

High-pitched squeaks echoed loudly in the small rock chamber, and I hid my face in my arms as the unseen creatures dropped off the walls all around us. Then, as quickly as they'd stirred, they were gone, darting up toward the surface.

The excitement left us all wide awake. "Boy, I sure wish we had the kind of radar guidance system bats do," Dad said enviously. "They're already up there in the moonlight, cruising around and eating mosquitoes."

"Why didn't we try to follow them, Dad?" Tim asked. "Or maybe catch one and tie something to its leg so it could lead us out?"

Dad laughed. "I don't think it would work, Tim. They're so fast we could never keep up with them, and if we caught one it would probably just flop around and die."

Now that the excitement was over, I was feeling really cold and thirsty. I hugged my knees tighter and tried not to think of the drinks sitting out in the truck. They might as well have been on Mars for all the good they did us.

And there was another problem, too, one that I'd been trying to ignore all afternoon. I had to go to the bathroom in the worst way.

Finally I told Dad. He said, "No problem, I'll just walk you over to a spot a little way from our rock. I don't want you to trip and hurt yourself in the dark."

I was relieved when he didn't even mention the plastic zip-lock bag. I guess he figured we were suffering enough.

After we got back to the rock, he took Tim next. We all tried to pretend to be deaf as well as blind, but it was still pretty embarrassing.

We talked for a while, then, about the spaghetti dinner we'd missed, and about the marshmallows we had planned to roast back at our campsite.

"When we get out of here I'm going to eat about five hamburgers and drink ten Dr. Peppers," Tim declared. I would've just settled for a big glass of water and a warm sleeping bag. I was so cold I could feel goose bumps prickling against the insides of my sleeves.

TUESDAY

I don't know what time it was when I dropped off to sleep again, but the next thing I remember was waking up to the noisy flapping of bat wings. It was 5 a.m. and they were returning to their roost. I listened as they squeaked and fluttered, attaching back onto the wall above my head. As soon as they were quiet again, I stood up and stretched.

"Ooh," I groaned, moving my shoulders up and down and rubbing my arms to warm them up. I felt stiff and achy—not really surprising considering I'd slept on a rock.

"You OK, Buddy?" Dad asked sleepily.

"Yeah, I guess. Just kind of sore."

Tim grunted and stood up. "I'm thirsty," he said, smacking his lips. "Do you think somebody'll come this morning, Dad?"

"I don't know, Tim. We'll just have to wait and see."

My eyes felt gritty and irritated, like they were full of dirt. When I rubbed at them I realized they *were* full of dirt, caked with the thick black dust we'd noticed the day before. "Ow," I grumbled as I tried to wipe it away. "This dust is really bad."

Dad led Tim and me over to the "bathroom," then we all sat back down on the big boulder. Dad sighed. "Well, this has been some lousy vacation so far, hasn't it? I'm really sorry I got you into this, guys."

I might've been mad at him if he wasn't already so mad at himself. "It just happened," I told him. "You didn't do it on purpose."

Tim was playing with his watch light, flicking it on and off. "I wish I had one of those watches with a video game," he said. "Then at least we could have something to do while we wait."

"That would be nice," Dad agreed.

I was thinking. "If we get out of here today or tomorrow, will we still have time to go rappelling?" I asked Dad. "You said you were going to teach us some of that stuff this trip."

"Sure, we can still do that. Pop and Grandma aren't expecting us at their house till Thursday night."

We took several long naps, just kind of drifting in and out of sleep. It helped pass the time, but after awhile I started getting a headache. I wasn't used to sleeping that much.

Tim and I talked about what we were going to do at Pop and Grandma's house. "Do you think they'll take us to Water Country or Busch Gardens this weekend?" Tim asked. "That was really fun last year."

I laughed, remembering the day we'd spent at the water park. "Remember how we were both too scared before to go down the biggest water slide? I'm gonna do it this time if we go there."

"Me too," Tim said, adding: "But remember how sore our feet were that night? I had about a million blisters from climbing all those stairs up to the slides. I could hardly walk for a couple days."

TUESDAY

"Oh, yeah! I'd forgotten about that. That was really bad."

We were quiet then, thinking about all the fun we'd had that day—the hot sun beating down, the noisy crowds, the exciting smells of water and chlorine and coconut suntan oil. For just a minute I was back there, far from New Trout Cave and the cold and the dark.

I sighed, leaning my head forward onto my knees. I was hungry and thirsty, and I wanted out of the cave. My chin started to quiver, and I bit my lip, hard. I was too old to cry.

It felt like days before nine o'clock finally came and the bats flapped away again for their nightly feeding.

10

Wednesday

When the bats returned, signaling that morning had come, I was too tired at first to care. Then I remembered—it was Wednesday, the day we were sure we'd be rescued!

I unfolded my legs and slipped down off the rock, but for a second I was dizzy, feeling like the whole cave was spinning around. "Whoa," I said, leaning back against the boulder. My voice sounded funny, kind of raspy, and I was shivering so hard I could barely talk.

"You OK, son?" Dad asked, reaching out a hand in the darkness to steady me. His voice was raspy, too.

"Yeah, I guess. I'm just a little dizzy."

Dad and I visited our bathroom, then went back to sit down. Tim was still asleep.

My mouth was really dry. I licked my lips, but it didn't help. My tongue was dry and swollen, and when I tried to swallow it hurt my throat. It took me a minute to realize my eyes were glued shut with dust again. It didn't really make much difference, but I peeled them apart and stretched my eyes wide open. I still couldn't see anything, but it *felt* a little better.

Tim started moving around right about then. "Dad?" he said sleepily. "Have the rescuers come yet?"

"No, son. But it's still pretty early in the morning. They probably won't show up until sometime this afternoon."

"Well, I hope they hurry. I'm getting really sick of this."

All morning, off and on, we took turns shouting, "Helloooo! We're in heeere!" We hadn't bothered to yell before, since hardly anybody went caveing during the week. But if someone was looking for us now it might make it easier for them to find us.

It was around 1 p.m. when Dad suddenly thought he saw a flicker of light. "Hey, did you see that?" he shouted excitedly. "I think somebody's coming with a lamp!"

Tim and I hadn't seen anything, but we all started shouting anyway. When we listened for an answer, though, there was just silence.

"Guess I must've been imagining things," Dad grumbled.

It happened again about three o'clock, only this time it was Tim who saw something. "Look over there!" he yelled, as if we could see where he was pointing. "I saw a light!"

We called again and again, but like before, there was no answer. "What's going on?" Dad wondered aloud. "Are we *all* seeing things?" It was kind of depressing thinking somebody was coming, then finding out nobody was there.

By 5 p.m. we were starting to figure it out. All three of us were now seeing little pinpoints of light, like flashbulbs popping in the distance, or faraway fireworks—but then we noticed we could still see them even when our eyes were closed. *Something was going wrong with our eyes.*

I was suddenly scared. "Dad, shouldn't the rescuers be here by now if they're coming?" I asked. "I mean, shouldn't we at least be able to *hear* them?"

Dad didn't answer for a long time, and when he did, his voice was so low I could hardly hear it. "I thought for sure somebody would report the truck by now, and come in after us. But it looks like we may have to spend another night in here."

Hearing him say that made my heart drop into my stomach. Ever since our lamps had gone out we'd been counting on the rescuers coming on Wednesday. If they didn't show up today, would they *ever* come?

Tim must have felt the same way, because he started crying. I felt a huge lump form in my own throat. Why did this have to happen to us?

We sat like that for a while, too discouraged to say much. Tim sobbed again and again, "I want to go home, Dad. I just want to go home." He sounded so little and helpless that I reached over and put my arm around him.

"It's gonna be all right, Tim," I told him, trying to sound like I knew what I was talking about. "If they don't come today, they'll for sure come tomorrow. Then we'll go to Pop and Grandma's for a big dinner."

He started to calm down a little, so I kept talking. "Hey, remember that 'Simpsons' episode last week —the one where Bart threw his sister's Christmas centerpiece in the fire and then ran away? Wasn't that great?"

Tim giggled half-heartedly. "Yeah, it was funny when they finally saw Bart on TV, eating dinner with the homeless people at that shelter."

We talked about a few of our other favorite shows: the "Cosby Show" and "Star Trek—The Next Generation." Still feeling kind of warm and big-brotherly, I said, "You know how I said you couldn't play that video game when I get it? Well, I guess I'll let you after all."

"Thanks!" Tim said, sounding almost normal. "I can't wait!"

It was really funny; if somebody had told me just a few days ago that I'd be sitting with my arm around Tim and telling him he could play my new video game, I'd have thought he was crazy. But now, with everything that had happened, it seemed like a perfectly normal thing to do. We all had to help each other.

It was only an hour later, though, that I suddenly noticed that Dad wasn't talking much—and that his breathing sounded funny.

"Are you OK, Dad?" I asked.

It took him a long time to answer. "Yeah, I'm fine," he said faintly. But his voice was just a whisper, and his breath was coming in sharp gasps.

Suddenly, I remembered the times earlier in the year when his heart had been bothering him and he hadn't been able to breathe. His pills had really helped. Then I realized he didn't have his pills with him. He'd left the bottle back at our campsite.

He hadn't had any of his medicine since we got stuck in the cave!

"Dad!" I said, scared. "You're still sitting up, aren't you?" Because of his warning about losing body heat on the cold rock, we'd spent the last three days sitting up, even when we slept.

"I'm up," Dad said with effort. He started to say something else, but stopped. Worried, I scooted over next to him. He was shivering so hard his arms and legs were jumping around by themselves.

Tears burned my eyes, and this time I didn't even try to stop them. *Please, God,* I prayed silently. *Please let somebody come soon.*

For a long time Dad gasped, struggling for air. Finally he whispered, "Buddy? Tim?"

"Right here," I told him, trying not to sound scared. He didn't sound good at all.

WEDNESDAY

"Listen, guys, I'm not doing all that great. I'm going to have to lie down for a minute."

"No!" I said, shocked. "No, Dad, you can't. You said it would just make us colder, and you're already shivering!"

He took another gasping breath. "Hush, Buddy. Just listen." He paused for another breath before going on: "If by any chance something happens to me tonight, I want you boys to take my shirt and overalls off and wrap yourselves up in them. It'll help keep you warm until the rescuers get here. Understand?"

"Oh, Dad!" I burst out. "Don't say that. You can't die. You just *can't!*" Tim and I both started sobbing this time.

Dad put his arms around us, hugging us to his chest. "I love you both so much. I'm just so sorry I got you into this." A moment later, he wearily slumped back onto the rock.

Tim and I both pulled at him, trying to lift him back up. "Dad!" I yelled. "Dad, get up!"

"Come on, Dad," Tim pleaded. "You can do it."

But Dad didn't answer; he just lay there, limp and gasping. "Oh, no," I moaned.

"Buddy, what are we going to do?" Tim said fearfully. Suddenly, I realized he was depending on *me* now.

I took a deep breath, trying to steady my voice. "Let's lie down on each side of him and put our arms across his chest. Maybe he'll be all right if we can keep him warm."

A moment later we were both stretched out alongside Dad on the cold boulder, hugging him tight. "Tim?" I said awkwardly. "I think we should try praying for him, too. You want to?"

"OK," he said.

I thought back to all the times I'd sat in Sunday School, only half-listening as my teacher read Bible stories. People back in Bible days always seemed to be praying and asking for miracles. I wasn't sure God still did that kind of stuff, but I was going to ask Him anyway.

"God," I prayed aloud, "Dad is really, really sick, and Tim and I don't know what to do." My voice broke, but this time I hardly noticed. "Can you please make him be OK? And can you please send somebody soon to get us out of here? We'd really appreciate it."

I hugged Dad hard, burying my face in his shoulder. It didn't seem like much of a prayer, but I couldn't think of anything else to say. I just hoped God understood.

The rock felt cold through my pants and shirt. As I lay there, shivering, holding onto Dad, I thought about all the times he had rushed home from work just so he could take me to some silly school meeting or football game—and all the times he'd understood when I'd really messed things up.

Like when I was seven, and accidentally broke

WEDNESDAY

our living room window with a toy truck I was swinging around. I'd been so scared I'd gone and hidden under my bed when I heard Dad come home.

But he just shook his head. "We all mess up sometimes," he told me, helping me slide back out from under the bed. "I don't think you'll make the same mistake again."

"You're just about the best dad in the whole world," I now whispered sleepily. "Please don't die."

I never heard the bats leave that night.

11

Outside the Cave

We didn't know it at the time, but Dad's guess that somebody would report our truck by Wednesday turned out to be pretty good.

At 1 p.m., just about the time Dad first started "seeing" the little flashes of light, a farmer was driving down the highway outside New Trout Cave on his way into town. He lived just a few miles away.

Over the last few days he had passed the cave several times, but at first he hadn't paid any attention to the truck—lots of people parked along the highway when they went camping or caving.

This time, though, he slowed down as he drove past, taking a good look. It suddenly struck him as odd that the truck hadn't moved for over three days.

The farmer ran his errands in town, and on the way home passed the truck again, still sitting beside the road. This time he stopped and jotted down the license plate number on a paper bag. A few minutes later, at home, he called the West Virginia State Police.

"Hey, listen, there's a little blue Mazda truck parked out along Highway 220 thet's been sittin' for sev'ral days," he told the trooper who answered the phone. "Reckon ya'll can ride out and take a look at it? It's got Flor'da plates on it. I wrote down the number."

Trooper Dave Lucas took down the information. "We'll check it out, sir. Thanks for calling in."

The trooper wasn't immediately worried by the call. There might be a good reason why a truck had stayed parked along the road for a few days—it might be broken down, or the driver might just be up in the hills enjoying a long camping trip. Until he could rule out several simple explanations, there was no reason for him to get excited.

He picked up the phone and called the police dispatch office. "Hi, it's Dave Lucas over here in Elkins. I need you to run a license check for me."

The dispatcher took down the information and told Lucas she'd call him right back. Then she typed the license number into a teletype, a machine like a personal computer. It was hooked up by phone to the state data center.

A few minutes later, words popped back up on the screen in front of her. She pushed a button to print out the information, then carefully ripped the page off the small printer. A moment later she was talking to Trooper Lucas again.

TRAPPED IN A CAVE!

"The Mazda truck belongs to a Gary Lutes in Tampa, Florida," she told him. "Here's his address."

Trooper Lucas took it down, then made a quick decision. "Let's go ahead and send a teletype to the Tampa police—maybe they know something about this Lutes guy."

"Sounds good," she said.

A few minutes later she sent off the teletype:

To: Tampa Police. From: West Virginia State Police. Vehicle belonging to Tampa resident Gary Lutes found abandoned along Highway 220. Please visit home of Lutes and try to determine his current whereabouts.

At 3 p.m. the Tampa police got the message from West Virginia and sent a deputy over to the house.

He knocked on the front door, but of course nobody answered. He was just about to leave when Mrs. Van Heertum pulled into her driveway next door.

The Van Heertums had lived next door to us for a long time, but I didn't really know them all that well. They were kind of old and talked with a funny accent—Dad said they were from New York. But they were nice and always smiled and waved if they saw us out in the yard. Mrs. Van Heertum usually picked up our newspapers and mail when we went away on short trips.

OUTSIDE THE CAVE

The policeman walked over as Mrs. Van Heertum got out of her car. "Excuse me, ma'am," he said, "but I was wondering if you might know where I can reach the Luteses."

Dad had told the Van Heertums that we were leaving on vacation. "They're out of town," she said. "I can't remember exactly where they said they were going—North Carolina or Virginia, somewhere like that. But I know Gary's brother has been checking on the house almost every night."

"Do you know his brother's name?"

Mrs. Van Heertum thought. "I've talked to him a few times, but I can't remember. Why? Is something wrong?"

The deputy explained, "Mr. Lutes' truck has been found abandoned in West Virginia, and we're trying to find out where he is. Does Mr. Lutes have a wife or kids who'd be with him?"

"His wife died a few years ago, but he has two little boys. I'm sure they're with him."

The deputy wrote down the information on a small pad, then thanked Mrs. Van Heertum. "If by any chance you hear from Mr. Lutes, please let us know. I'm going to leave my card on their front door."

After the policeman left, Mrs. Van Heertum remembered something she should have mentioned to him—we almost never used our front door. We always went in and out through the garage. She decided to leave another note on our garage door, just in case.

TRAPPED IN A CAVE!

She found a piece of paper and a marker and wrote a note in big black letters:

TO GARY OR HIS BROTHER—Please call the next-door neighbors immediately. Gary's truck was found in West Virginia, and the police want to know where he is.

"There!" she said as she taped the note to the front of our garage. "They won't miss seeing *that!*"

But late that afternoon a bad thunderstorm suddenly blew into Tampa. Lightning crashed every couple seconds, and so much rain fell the streets looked like rivers. Whenever it rained hard like that, it got so deep people got out canoes and went rafting right in the streets.

Uncle Jim had planned to stop by our house again on his way home from work. But now, with the storm being so bad, he decided to go straight home.

"It won't hurt to skip this one night," he told Aunt Jean. "Gary won't care."

He didn't know that, at that very moment, Dad was gasping, barely breathing as he lay slumped back on a cold rock deep in New Trout Cave.

12

Thursday

I woke up slowly, my head hurting. For a second I thought I'd just been having a bad dream about being trapped in New Trout. I'd been cold and hungry, and nobody had come for us. And there was something else, something about Dad . . .

He was dying.

Suddenly, I remembered what had happened—and realized I was sitting up again, my arms around my knees, instead of lying next to Dad to keep him warm.

In a panic, I felt around wildly in the dark. "Dad! Dad, are you all right?"

"I'm right here, son." Relieved, I reached my hand toward Dad's voice and touched his shoulder. He was sitting up again.

Tim was now moving around. "Dad?" he said, his voice barely a whisper. We all sounded funny, our voices deep and raspy.

"I'm OK, Tim," Dad said. "I don't know what happened, but I'm feeling a lot better now."

I suddenly remembered something. "Tim and I prayed for you last night, when we were scared you were going to die."

"Thanks," Dad said softly. "You guys must really know how to pray."

For a few minutes we just sat there, too relieved to even talk. We'd been so discouraged the night before, but now it was like we had another chance.

My eyes were glued shut with dust again, but this time I decided to just leave them. What difference did it make? In a way it was easier to keep them closed where I wasn't always straining to see. It's *supposed* to be dark when your eyes are closed.

I tried to stand up then, to stretch. But the minute I slid down off the boulder my legs buckled. I had to grab Dad to keep from falling down.

"I think we'd all better stay on the rock from now on," he said. "We're too weak to move around." It really didn't matter now, anyway; none of us had to go to the bathroom any more. I guess when you don't eat or drink anything for a couple days you just quit.

My mouth was dry and sore, and my lips felt puffy, like I'd been hit in the mouth. My tongue was like sandpaper and my taste buds stuck up in little dry bumps. I cleared my throat, trying to get rid of the dry tickle from all the dust.

"Isn't tonight when we were supposed to get to Grandma and Pop's house?" I asked. "They'll for sure know something is wrong if we don't show up."

THURSDAY

"That's right," Dad agreed. "And even if it's late when they call the police, it won't matter. It's just as easy to do a cave rescue at night as it is during the day."

He quickly added, "But I'm still hoping somebody'll show up earlier today."

"Me, too," I said sincerely.

It was still early morning; the bats must've woke me up when they came back into the cave. I pressed the light button on my watch, then remembered I'd have to pry my eyes open to see the time. I decided it wasn't worth the effort.

Huddled on the rock, I tried to think about something besides how cold and thirsty I felt. I was shivering so hard all the time now that the muscles in my stomach and arms were tight and sore. I decided I'd never complain again about how hot Florida got in the summer.

Since there wasn't anything better to do, I leaned my head on my knees and drifted back off to sleep.

I dreamed at first that I was at the school playground, playing football with James. "Run out!" I told him, waving the ball. "I'll throw you a long pass!"

But when James put his hands up for me to toss the ball, I couldn't move—I was frozen like a statue on the playground. From far away I could hear James calling my name, again and again, but I couldn't answer him. My lips wouldn't move.

TRAPPED IN A CAVE!

Then, suddenly, I was sitting in our living room at home watching Saturday cartoons and holding a paper plate piled with pepperoni pizza. It smelled delicious, and I was just about to pick up a piece when Uncle Jim walked in. "You can't have that, Buddy," he said. "It's not dinnertime."

I woke up moaning, still almost able to smell the pizza. It made the darkness and cold seem even worse.

Even though I knew it was probably a bad idea, I asked Dad, "What do you think Grandma is making for dinner tonight?" If I couldn't have anything to eat, I wanted to at least *talk* about food.

"Well, you know Grandma. She's probably already made a couple pies for us, and she'll be cooking some chicken or maybe a big beef roast." He sighed. "I sure wish we had some of that now."

Tim groaned. "I do, too. Do you think we'll be out in time to still get there tonight for dinner?"

"I kind of doubt it, Tim. When we get out I'm not going to want to drive for hours before I eat. I think we'll just go to the first restaurant we can find and order one of everything. I feel like I could eat for days without slowing down."

I finally unstuck my eyes, then, so I could see what time it was. It was almost noon.

"Maybe the rescuers are already looking for us now," I said hopefully, inspired by all that talk of food. "Should we take turns yelling again just in case?"

THURSDAY

Dad thought about it. "I don't guess it would hurt. But let's not wear ourselves out this time—we need to save our strength as much as possible."

I shouted until I got tired, then I drifted back off to sleep. Dad was right; we were so weak we got tired easily, and yelling made me cough. It felt good to rest.

I napped on and off all afternoon, waking up just long enough each time to check my watch. I kept imagining what Grandma was doing each time as she got ready for us to show up for dinner: checking the roast, setting the table, making the iced tea . . .

We had planned to be at Grandma and Pop's by around six o'clock. By seven, I was picturing how worried they must be.

"Where are Gary and the boys?" Grandma would be saying. "I just know something must be wrong."

"Maybe we should call the police," Pop would suggest.

"Good idea. Let's do it right now."

By 7:30 p.m. I could almost hear the sirens screaming down the highway toward New Trout Cave. When they saw our truck sitting there, they'd know we were inside. Before long we'd hear them calling us, or see their lamps reflecting on the cave walls.

But at 9:30 p.m. when the bats flapped away again, we were still waiting in the cold darkness.

"Where *are* they?" I finally asked in frustration.

"Shouldn't Pop and Grandma have called some-body by now?"

"I'm sure they have, Buddy," Dad said wearily. "It's probably just taking a while to get all the rescuers together."

Tim had been quiet for a long time. But now he suddenly spoke: "Dad, who's that standing over there?"

For a split second I stared all around, hoping to see a rescuer who'd silently slipped in. But as usual, there was nothing but darkness.

"What are you talking about, Tim?" Dad said quietly. "Where do you see somebody?"

Tim mumbled something, then started cough-ing really hard. I could hear Dad patting his back, trying to help him stop.

"Tim?" Dad sounded worried as Tim kept cough-ing, almost gagging. Suddenly I was worried, too. What was wrong with him?

Finally Tim settled down. "Buddy?" he said in a tiny voice.

"Yeah?" I answered. I hoped he wasn't seeing another strange person standing in the dark.

"Are you really going to let me play your new video game when we get out of here?"

I was so relieved I almost laughed. "Yeah, Tim, whenever you want." I didn't care any more that he always followed me around and got me in trouble with Dad. I just wanted him to be all right.

A few minutes later he started coughing again,

only this time it was even worse. It sounded like he wasn't getting any air.

"Come on, Tim," Dad said over and over. "Try to calm down and take a deep breath. The rescuers are probably on their way right now."

Scared, I reached over and patted Tim on the shoulder. "Everything's gonna be OK," I told him, hoping I sounded more convincing than I felt. "You'll see."

When Tim finally stopped coughing, he mumbled something about a dog. I suddenly felt ice cold.

There was something wrong—*really wrong*—with Tim.

We didn't know it then, but we'd come close to being rescued three different times that day. If things had gone just a little differently, somebody would've found out we were in trouble.

The first time was that morning, when Trooper Rick Gillespie came on duty at the police office in Elkins.

The teletype Dave Lucas had sent off to Tampa the day before had never been answered, so Gillespie decided to send off another message:

Still waiting for information on Gary Lutes. Please respond immediately.

But before he could hear back from the Tampa police, another emergency came up—a local man called in to say that his wife had left their house early that morning to take a short walk and had never come back.

"She has heart problems," he told Trooper Gillespie. "I'm afraid something has happened. She could be lying out there somewhere needing help."

Gillespie quickly called together a search party to try to find the woman. They were still looking for her late that afternoon when the teletype finally came in from Tampa.

Re: Gary Lutes. According to neighbor, he is on vacation with two young sons. No further information at this time.

When Trooper Gillespie read the message, he shook his head. He had a feeling the family was in some kind of trouble, but until he found the lady he *knew* was missing, he couldn't spare any men for a second search. It would just have to wait.

The second time we came close to being rescued was when we didn't show up at Grandma and Pop's house for dinner. Just like I imagined, they got worried and thought about calling the police.

But then they decided that maybe we were just camping out for an extra day. "Let's give them till tomorrow," Pop said. "They're probably just having such a good time they forgot to call."

Our third, and last, chance was that night, when Uncle Jim had planned to go check our house. Mrs. Van Heertum's note was still taped to

THURSDAY

the garage door where he would've been sure to see it.

But the storm from the day before was still howling, and the streets all still flooded. Uncle Jim decided to put off checking on the house for just one more day.

13

Friday

Thursday night seemed to go on forever. When the bats finally flapped back in at 4:30 a.m. on Friday, I hardly noticed—I felt numb, like I was wrapped up in cotton. My chest ached each time I breathed.

Tim had coughed and moaned all night, and now I was coughing, too. The thick black dust made the sides of my throat stick together each time I tried to swallow. I felt like I was suffocating.

"I'm thirsty," I said. My voice came out in a whispered croak, and my lips were cracked and peeling, puffed up to almost twice their normal size. My tongue was thick and swollen, like a dry stick; as I talked, I could actually *hear* it rasping against the roof of my mouth.

Nobody had come for us. A hundred times during the night I thought I heard someone calling my name, but each time it was just my imagination. Nobody had come.

I sat in a daze now, listening to Tim's faint breathing. He sounded like Dad had on Wednesday, gasping for air. Every few minutes he went into another coughing fit.

I had tried to keep him talking, afraid that if he fell asleep he might quit breathing. Half the time he just said crazy things—complaining that his camp cot was ripped, or that it wasn't his turn to wash the dishes. I kept reminding him that we were sitting in a dark cave and that there weren't any dishes to wash, but I don't think he even heard me.

"I wish we'd never come here," I said, startled to realize I'd spoken my thought aloud. Maybe I was going crazy, too.

Dad didn't say anything; he just put his arm around me. I felt bad for saying that and making him feel even worse.

I was so tired I could hardly think. I leaned my head against Dad's shoulder, just meaning to rest for a minute, but I must have dozed off.

Suddenly I was back at home, leaning back in Dad's big, soft recliner. I wanted to watch TV, so I picked up the remote control and pressed the "on" button. But nothing happened.

I tried again, pushing the button over and over, but it still wouldn't work. The TV screen stayed black.

"Dad!" I yelled. "The remote control is busted. Can you come fix it?" My voice came out in a hoarse whisper, so I tried again: "Dad!"

"Buddy, I'm right here," Dad said in my ear. His

voice was hoarse, too. "Wake up, son. There's no television here. You must be dreaming."

I sat up then, my heart sinking when I felt the cold rock under me and remembered where I was. *This* was a bad dream.

It seemed like only a few minutes later that I felt Dad suddenly jump. "Look at that!" he said excitedly. "Why didn't we see that before?"

"What?" I asked, confused. I didn't see anything.

"The Coke machine!" Dad said. "It's right across the room; don't you see it? We can finally get a drink."

My chin started quivering. I couldn't take much more of this.

"Dad, there's no Coke machine in here," I told him shakily. "You're seeing things."

"No, I'm not. I'm telling you, it's right there!"

I said slowly: "We're sitting in a dark cave. Even if there *was* a Coke machine, you couldn't see it."

That seemed to make him think, so I quit talking. Whether he believed me or not, I was too tired to argue with him any more.

By now somebody *must* be looking for us. Pop and Grandma knew we wouldn't just not show up at their house. Maybe they were still trying to figure out exactly where we were. I wished we had told somebody where we were going.

I let my mind drift, thinking back to when I was younger, and when Mom was still alive. I could suddenly remember her face clearly, even the little gap that showed between her front teeth when she smiled. She was a lot like Dad, always taking us places—bike riding, or to the park, or for a picnic. At night she used to read to Tim and me before we went to bed.

I smiled, remembering the afternoon I won second place in the Cub Scout "Pinewood Derby" race. Dad and I had built the little model car in our garage out of some old wood, and that Saturday I couldn't wait to get home to tell Mom about the race. I was eight years old.

By then Mom was already really sick, lying in bed with lots of tubes in her arms and nose. She couldn't talk, but when I held up my trophy her whole face lit up in a big smile.

Four days later, she died.

The memory made a lump rise suddenly in my throat. For the first time in a long time I missed Mom—not just because I wanted a mom to do things for me, but because I wanted *her*. Why did these things have to happen?

Tim started coughing and choking again, getting weaker and weaker. I scooted over next to him and put my arm around him. *Please, God, help Tim breathe,* I prayed again and again as he choked and gagged. Each time, he slowly settled down.

It was about 5 p.m. when he finally said, "Dad? They're not going to come, are they?"

Dad could barely talk, his voice was so hoarse.

"Yes, Tim, they are. By now they're definitely on their way."

But somehow, it just didn't sound real this time. We sat for a minute without talking, then Tim sighed.

"I just wish I'd gotten to go to fifth grade. I was really looking forward to that."

When he said that, something inside me just seemed to burst. I started sobbing, unable to hold it all in any longer.

Dad groaned, then I heard him start to cry, too. When he put his arms out, Tim and I grabbed onto him and each other.

"I love you boys," Dad sobbed. "I love you so much. I'm so sorry I brought you here."

"I love you, too, Dad," I cried. Tim added, "You're the best dad there ever was." We stayed huddled like that for a long time, just holding on to each other and crying.

I don't know how long we stayed like that, but finally we all quieted down. Tim started coughing again, and this time he almost couldn't get his breath back. Afterward, he leaned back against Dad, too tired to talk.

Even if rescuers *were* on their way, I suddenly knew it would be too late.

Early that Wednesday morning, Dad had come in and sat down on my bed. "Buddy?" he said quietly. As soon as I looked up at him, I knew. His eyes were red and swollen.

"Mom is gone," he said. "She never woke up. She passed on early this morning."

He put his arm around me. "It's just the three of us now."

I thought about that for a few minutes, wondering about some things. I finally said, "Dad? What will it be like to die?"

I almost expected him to shush me, but he didn't. He just took a shaky breath.

"Well," he said slowly, "at first hypothermia will make us feel very sleepy, so sleepy we won't be able to keep our eyes open. Then after a while we'll just slowly lose consciousness. Eventually, I guess, our hearts will just stop beating."

I thought about that. *It didn't really sound so bad—kind of like going to sleep and not waking up. That must have been the way it was with Mom.*

"What happens then?" Tim asked.

Dad said softly, "We'll be in Paradise. No more hunger, no more thirst, no more darkness. And the four of us—us and your mother—will all be together again."

We hugged again, this time not even crying. Suddenly, I didn't feel scared or worried any more. I wasn't going to get to go to college or get a job, but at least I'd still be with Mom and Dad and Tim. That was all that really counted.

Before Mom died I used to picture heaven like on TV, with clouds and harps and things. But at her funeral the pastor talked about it being a "heavenly city" with mansions and streets made of gold, and even a river and fruit trees. That made a lot more sense to me—I knew Mom would hate a place where all she could do was sit around. I felt better knowing she had a nice place to live and good food to eat.

And now, before long, I'd be with her.

It was 7 p.m. when Dad, Tim, and I finally lay back on the rock, no longer worried about getting cold. After sitting up for five straight days, it felt good to stretch out. We were all so tired.

14

Help on
the Way

It seems strange that at almost the same time we were deciding it was hopeless, things were finally starting to happen.

First, at around noon on Friday, the lady who was missing was found in some woods near her house. She'd had a heart attack. By the time they found her, it was too late to do anything.

Trooper Gillespie called the woman's husband, then told several of his men: "You'd better get some lunch now, while you can. We're probably going to be starting another search right away."

He drove out to make sure that our truck was still sitting by the highway, and while he was there he decided to get out and look it over. He immediately spotted the sticker Dad had put on the back window—a little black bat, a symbol of the National Speleological Society.

Gillespie looked up the hillside, suddenly realizing how close the truck was to the three caves.

"That's got to be it," he said to himself. "I bet they're in one of those caves."

He drove back to his office and called the NSS's Field House—a kind of meeting place for cavers. There was a big caving convention that week, so he thought somebody should be there. He wanted to double check that Dad really was a caver.

A few minutes later a man at the Field House was checking his records. "Yep, here it is," he told Gillespie. "Gary Lutes, with an address in Tampa. He's been an NSS member for almost twenty years."

Trooper Gillespie thought for a moment, trying to make a plan. "Can you help me track down some information about this guy, maybe find somebody who knows him? It'll make it easier to find him and his kids if we know which cave they were going in."

"We'll do our best," the man replied. "I'll start making some calls right now."

While Gillespie started pulling together a full-scale police search, the man at the Field House called some other cavers who lived in Tampa.

"Do you know a guy named Gary Lutes?" he asked each of them. "We think he might be in trouble in a cave up here in West Virginia."

None of them knew Dad—he hardly even went to their meetings. But one woman, Toni Williams, offered to call all the "Lutes" in the Tampa phone book, hoping to find one of Dad's relatives.

HELP ON THE WAY

"I'll call you back if I find out anything," she said.

At that very moment, Uncle Jim was just starting home from work. The storm had finally quit, and he was planning to stop by our house on the way.

The first thing he saw when he pulled into our driveway was the paper taped to the garage door. He jumped out of the car and quickly read the note from Mrs. Van Heertum, then pulled it off and read it again:

TO GARY OR HIS BROTHER—Please call the next-door neighbors immediately. Gary's truck was found in West Virginia, and the police want to know where he is.

Hoping there was some mistake, he ran next door and rang the doorbell, but the Van Heertums weren't home. Panicking, Uncle Jim ran back to our house and pulled out the electric garage door opener, planning to use our phone to check with the police.

But the door wouldn't open; the thunderstorm had burned it out the day before. Uncle Jim pounded on the door in frustration, then finally jumped back into his car and sped home.

The phone was ringing when he rushed in. Aunt Jean answered it, then held it out to Uncle Jim.

"It's somebody named Toni Williams, with the

NSS," she told him, looking worried. "She says Gary's truck has been sitting by a highway in West Virginia for the last *five days!*"

Uncle Jim snatched the phone, his face suddenly pale. "Hello?" he said. "This is Jim, Gary's brother..."

Up in Virginia, Pop and Grandma were also worried. That afternoon, they had finally called the state police to ask if there had been any accidents involving our family. They'd been waiting by the phone ever since.

About 7:15 p.m., Uncle Jim called. "Did Gary and the boys ever show up there?" he asked.

"No, they sure didn't," Grandma told him. "And it isn't like Gary not to call if he's going to be late."

"The West Virginia police found his truck on a highway by some caves," Uncle Jim explained. "They want to know for sure if he's overdue anywhere."

"You tell them yes, he is," Grandma said. "He's over a day late now getting here."

Uncle Jim called Toni Williams, then the West Virginia State Police.

"There's definitely something wrong," he told Trooper Gillespie. "My brother never showed up at his in-laws' house last night."

Trooper Gillespie sighed. "I was afraid of that. I've already got a police search organized, but now that we know for sure that they're missing I'll call in the NCRC—the National Cave Rescue Commission. They should be able to help us."

He added, "It would really help if we knew which cave they were in. Did he mention his plans to you?"

"No, nothing specific. He just said something about caves 'up around Franklin.' That could be any of them!"

After Trooper Gillespie got off the phone with Uncle Jim, he called a man named John Hempel, with the NCRC. "We've got a man and his two sons who are missing," he said. "Can you send out some trained cavers to help us search the three caves close to where their truck was found?"

"No problem," Mr. Hempel said. "We've got over a hundred cavers in town for a convention. You'll have all the help you need!"

Within minutes, Trooper Gillespie was heading back out along Highway 220 toward the three caves. He planned to set up a command post just outside the entrances to try to keep the search organized. He had brought a box of walkie-talkies for the searchers to use.

It as almost 9 p.m. when he pulled off the highway and parked beside our truck. Several cavers arrived at the same time.

"Heard you needed some help!" one of them called as he got out of his car. He had a backpack slung over one shoulder and was carrying a hard hat under one arm.

"Sure do," Gillespie said. "I appreciate you coming out like this."

As they started up the steep hill together, bats began to pour out of the three caves. Gillespie looked up as they darted back and forth overhead, chasing mosquitoes in the moonlight. "I've never liked those things," he said.

At the top of the hill they all peered at the cavers' log book in the small shelter. "Look, here's where they signed in!" said Gillespie, pointing to Dad's signature. "It's dated last Monday."

"That's a long time to be trapped," one caver said. "I bet something happened to the father, and the two boys had no way to get back out. It's happened before."

By then the highway was getting crowded with cars. The cavers were divided into three groups to do a "hasty search," a quick check of the main tunnels of each cave. Trooper Gillespie gave each group a walkie-talkie.

"Be careful," he said as they started into the caves. "We don't need for anybody else to get hurt."

A few minutes later his walkie-talkie crackled as the groups reported in:

We're moving back in Hamilton, but no sign of them anywhere in the main tunnel.

Nothing so far here in Trout.

We're almost to the Big Room in New Trout. We'll check the sign-in book there to see if they went into the Maze.

HELP ON THE WAY

But when they looked at the book, lying on a rock just a few feet from where Dad, Tim, and I had sat, our names weren't there—we had never seen it.

Nope, nothing here. But at least now we know they weren't here in New Trout—they must have gone into one of the other caves. We're on our way back out.

Trooper Gillespie was thinking. "Let's go back down to the highway where the Lutes' truck is parked," he told one of the searchers. "Maybe they left something inside it to show which cave they planned to explore."

The truck was locked, but Trooper Gillespie gave orders for another police officer to break into it. He slid a thin piece of metal in around the edge of the door and managed to flip up the door lock.

The minutes Trooper Gillespie opened the door and leaned inside, he wrinkled his nose. "Something in here smells really bad," he said.

He saw the cooler and lifted the lid. Our sandwiches had been sitting there since Monday, and they'd all gone rotten. He quickly slammed the lid back down.

"These folks definitely planned to be back out here days ago," Trooper Gillespie said. "Let's just hope they left us some clue about where they went."

But of course, there was nothing in our truck to show we'd gone in New Trout. After looking around carefully, Trooper Gillespie locked our truck again and climbed back up the hill.

TRAPPED IN A CAVE!

For the next two hours, the rescuers walked and crawled through Hamilton and Trout Caves. Each time a passage was searched and found empty, they'd leave a "cairn," a stack of small rocks, in the entrance with a note sticking out the top, saying: "Checked by Trout Team #1" or "Hamilton Team #3." That way, nobody wasted time checking the same tunnel twice.

Outside, more and more cavers kept showing up. By midnight there were over a hundred people milling around the cave entrances. Trooper Gillespie stayed at his command post, picking new rescue teams every now and then to switch with the ones coming out of the caves. He didn't want any of the rescuers to get so tired that they'd accidentally hurt themselves.

Finally, John Hempel, the NCRC coordinator, walked up with Martin Hardy, a caver who was a land surveyor, just like Dad. Mr. Hempel was a big man with a bald spot on top; Mr. Hardy was tall and skinny with curly red hair and a mustache. They'd both helped in lots of other rescues, and Mr. Hempel even taught classes about how to rescue people in caves. Sometimes he flew to other countries to help when big caving accidents happened.

Mr. Hempel introduced himself to Trooper Gillespie, then asked, "Where have you checked so far?"

"We've been concentrating mostly on Trout and Hamilton. The Lutes hadn't signed the inside register in New Trout, so we figured they were probably in one of the other caves."

Mr. Hempel thought about that. "Well, just to be safe, why don't I take a small team into New Trout to look around? I'm pretty familiar with it; I took some cavers back into the Maze just a couple weeks ago when I was teaching a rescue course. It's easy to get lost in there; that's for sure."

"OK, sounds good," said Gillespie. "Who do you want to take with you?"

Mr. Hempel looked over at Martin Hardy, who was wearing a bright orange jumpsuit. "You want to go with me?" Mr. Hempel asked him.

"Sure," he said. "And here comes Rick Backus—he might want to go, too."

Mr. Backus grinned as he walked up. "Hi there," he boomed in a deep voice. "You need more help?" He was a big man with a dark, bushy beard.

"Yeah, come on with Marty and me. We're going to check out New Trout just in case the Lutes somehow missed the inside register."

They became "New Trout Team #1." Trooper Gillespie handed them a walkie-talkie.

"I hope you guys have better luck in finding the Lutes than we've had so far," he told them. "I'm just afraid it might already be too late."

"We'll do our best," Mr. Hempel said. "Come on, let's get started."

The three men started into New Trout, Mr. Hempel leading the way. When they reached the Big

Room, he pointed over to the low tunnel that led into the Maze.

"That's where we need to go," he said. "If they're stuck anywhere in New Trout, it'll be in there."

One by one, they crawled into the narrow passage and started slowly working their way into the Maze. Every now and they they stopped and shouted, "Gary! Mr. Lutes! Can you hear us?" When they got no answer they kept going.

They had already worked their way through a number of tunnels when Mr. Hempel's headlamp suddenly lit up something bright red in the passage ahead. He hurried forward and picked up the red object.

It was our backpack.

"This is it!" he yelled, opening the pack to look inside. He pulled out Tim's and my water bottles, labeled with our names. "Tim and Buddy," he read aloud. "Those must be the two Lutes boys! They're definitely somewhere here in New Trout."

They were too deep in the cave to call out on the walkie-talkie, so Rick Backus volunteered to run back out to let the others know.

"OK. While you're doing that, Marty and I will keep trying to locate them," Mr. Hempel said. "They can't be too far from their pack."

The two men climbed down the steep drop-off near the backpack, figuring we must've gone that way. After they squeezed through the same little crack we'd squeezed through five days before, they

HELP ON THE WAY

started yelling again. "Gary! Buddy! Tim! Answer if you can hear us!"

When they'd stopped and called for about the twentieth time without getting an answer, Mr. Hempel shook his head.

"I'm getting a bad feeling about this. They should be able to hear us. *Why aren't they answering?*"

Mr. Hardy had just been thinking the same thing. "If they've been stuck in here five days without food or water," he said grimly, "it might already be too late."

15

Seeing
Stars

I was drifting, half-asleep, feeling like somebody was pushing a heavy weight down on my chest. I had to fight each time I took a breath. It hurt so bad that I tried to take only little breaths each time.

Every now and then I'd hear Dad or Tim mumble something in the darkness, but a few times I heard other people talking—my friend James or my English teacher.

"You want to go ride bikes?" James asked me. But I was too tired to answer. *Doesn't he know I don't have my bike with me?*

And then there was my teacher, Mrs. O'Reilly. "You need to study for your vocabulary quiz tomorrow," she told me. "It counts as two grades."

"I already took that test," I said aloud, then jumped when I heard my own voice. Why was I talking to Mrs. O'Reilly? She hadn't come to the cave with us, had she?

I was so tired. *Why don't they all just leave me alone?*

SEEING STARS

I was almost asleep again when I heard a faraway voice calling my name. "Leave me alone," I mumbled. "I don't want to talk."

A moment later I heard it again, only this time it was louder. "Gary! Buddy! Can you hear us?" I still ignored it.

Beside me, though, I suddenly heard Tim gasp and sit up. "Hey!" he said, his voice just a hoarse whisper. "Hey, somebody's calling us!"

That woke me up at last. If Tim could hear it, too, it must be real! I sat up, feeling sick and dizzy. "Gary Lutes!" the voice called. "Can you hear us?" Dad sat up, coughing from the effort.

I cleared my throat and yelled, "We're in here! We're over here!" Shouting made a sharp pain cut through my chest, but I didn't care. I just hoped we weren't all hearing things again.

Dad and Tim started yelling then, too. A minute later we heard the voice calling back, "Keep shouting! We're almost there!"

When we finally saw a faint light reflecting off the cave walls, at first I couldn't believe it. All the days we'd watched and waited, hoping to see someone coming with a light. I was afraid any second it would disappear, just another dream.

But this time the light kept growing, getting brighter and brighter. And then, suddenly, two men stepped around the corner into the room where we were sitting.

At first I couldn't see their faces—just two blinding lights, like the headlights on a car. I squinted, my eyes hurting.

Dad slowly stood up, hanging onto the rock to keep from falling down. "Thank God," he whispered. "Thank God you found us. Do you have any water?"

"Right here," Mr. Hempel said, pulling out a small bottle. "But you can only have a few sips. Any more than that could make you sick."

He handed Tim the bottle first, keeping his hand on it so he could pull it away if he had to. While I waited for my turn, I looked over at Dad.

Now that my eyes were starting to adjust to the light, I could finally see a little better. Dad looked back at me, and suddenly we both grinned. Both our faces were solid black, smeared with the thick cave dust. Even our *teeth* were black!

Then, at last, it was my turn to drink. I had a hard time making my cracked lips fit around the top of the bottle, but somehow I managed. I held the water in my mouth for a second, just enjoying how it felt, then I let it slide down my throat. I've never tasted anything so good in my life.

Mr. Hempel let me have another little sip, then he handed the bottle to Dad. Tim and I sat, waiting to be told what we should do next.

"Well, are you guys about ready to get out of here?" Mr. Hardy finally asked.

"You bet," I said. My voice wasn't as raspy as it

had been before. I guess that little sip of water had made all the difference.

"Let's see if you can stand up," Mr. Hempel said, grabbing my arm to help. I slowly slid down off the rock. For a second I felt really dizzy, but he held me up.

"Can you walk?" he asked me.

"I think so," I replied. I didn't much like the idea of somebody trying to carry me across all those loose rocks and maybe dropping me. I'd rather take my chances walking.

Mr. Hardy was helping Tim up. "Ow!" Tim shouted as he tried to stand. "My heel hurts *bad*." He was holding up his right foot.

"Do you think you can walk on it?" Mr. Hardy asked.

"I don't know. I guess I'll try."

We started out, Mr. Hempel leading the way. He was half-carrying Tim as he limped along beside him.

Mr. Hardy walked beside me, keeping one hand kind of under my arm. "'You doing OK?" he asked.

"Uh-huh," I said. I was having to concentrate on each step, telling my legs to keep moving. They almost felt like they weren't a part of me anymore, it had been so long since I'd used them. I kept stepping down where I thought the ground would be, but my foot just kept going. It felt really strange, like I was wading through the floor.

We walked for about five minutes, then I had to

rest. My chest was aching and I was breathing hard, like I'd been running. I couldn't seem to get enough air.

Mr. Hardy patted me on the back. "You're doing fine," he said. "Hang in there."

It took forever for us to reach the narrow squeeze near the ledge where we'd left the pack, and by then my legs were trembling so badly I wasn't sure I could crawl through. But Dad and Mr. Hardy helped me, and soon I was on the other side, crawling back up onto the rock ledge.

It was funny how unreal everything seemed now that we were finally on our way out. We'd been so excited a few days before when we first thought we saw lights; but now it was like it was all happening to somebody else. I kept half-expecting to wake up and find out we were still sitting in the dark.

We had only gone a little farther when Rick Backus showed back up. "They're pulling everybody out of the other two caves now, and they've got an ambulance waiting outside."

As we started forward again he raised an eyebrow when he saw how badly Tim was limping. A moment later he was swinging him up onto his back.

"There you go, young fella," he said. "I think you and me are going to head out of here and leave these old folk behind. How about it?"

Tim smiled a little. "Sounds OK to me."

Mr. Backus looked back at me and winked, then

ducked his head and started off with Tim. For just a second I wished somebody would offer to carry me after all. I was feeling sick to my stomach, and I still couldn't breathe very well. I wasn't sure I was going to be able to walk all the way out.

"Can we stop and rest for a minute?" I asked. "I don't feel so good."

Mr. Hardy put his arm around my shoulders and tried to help me along. "Let's keep going as long as we can. We need to get you out to the ambulance where you can lie down and be comfortable. It's only a little farther."

Finally, we crawled out into the Big Room. Mr. Hempel pointed to the small sign-in book lying on a rock.

"If you'd just signed the New Trout register before you went into the Maze, we could've found you guys hours ago. Everybody thought you must be in one of the other caves."

Dad shook his head. "We never saw it," he explained. "We sat in here and ate a snack and even refueled our lamps, but we never noticed any book. I definitely would've signed it if we had."

About that time Rick Backus popped in again. I don't know how he had so much energy; I was so tired I wanted to cry. When Mr. Hardy said, "Time to get moving again," I just sat there.

"I can't go any farther," I said, rubbing my aching chest and queasy stomach. This was almost worse than sitting in the dark.

TRAPPED IN A CAVE!

Mr. Backus walked over to me. "Come on, now, it's only a little way now. We'll help you." He and Mr. Hardy practically picked me up and stood me back on my feet.

For the rest of the way out they walked on each side of me, almost dragging me along. When we finally reached the tunnel leading to the entrance, Mr. Backus pointed ahead.

"See all those people standing there with all the lights?" he said. "That's the outside. We're almost there."

I stumbled forward, concentrating on making my feet keep moving—step, step, step. I hardly noticed where I was until I suddenly smelled the warm, clean scent of grass.

I looked up then, discovering to my surprise that I was standing on the hillside just outside the cave. Police and ambulance lights were flashing everywhere, and people were milling all around. The warm summer air felt good, like a blanket.

Dad was just behind me. We both stopped for a minute, staring up at the night sky. It was clear and full of stars.

I felt a lump form in my throat. *Thank You*, I said silently, still staring up. *Thank You for letting them find us.*

Dad must have been feeling the same thing, because he just stood there with me, not even talking. But finally he looked down at me.

SEEING STARS

"You know," he said, his voice kind of choking. "We almost died in there. I really messed up."

I reached over to squeeze his hand, suddenly knowing just what to say.

"It's OK, Dad," I told him. "We all mess up sometimes."

16

One
Year Later

It's strange, looking back now, to remember everything that happened last summer. In some ways it seems like it all must have happened to somebody else, and not to me.

But there are plenty of things around to remind me that it really *did* happen. Like Dad and Tim, for starters.

Tim still follows me around all the time and causes trouble, but I don't mind it as much as I used to. Every time I start to get mad at him, I remember how I felt in the cave when I thought he was going to die. I guess I never really knew until then how much I—well—*loved* him, although I still won't tell *him* that.

And then there's Miss Kitty, the little black kitten we found after we got back home. She was lying out in our backyard, sick and starved.

"I guess we know just what she feels like, don't we?" Dad said, feeling how her bones stuck out along her sides. We took her inside and fed her and took care of her, and before long she was fat and shiny.

Miss Kitty likes to poke her nose under the edge of our living room rug and wiggle her way under it, then bump around the floor like a little rug ghost. And whenever we feed her, she drags her food out of her dish and eats it with her paws, lying on her side. I figure that must just be her way of enjoying good food.

And speaking of enjoying food, that's one thing I'll never forget—our first meal after New Trout.

After we finally got out of the cave, Dad and I walked down to the highway where the ambulance was waiting. Tim was already there.

When we got to the ambulance, somebody handed each of us a giant glass of Coke. I buried my face in mine, gulping it down, letting it wash away some of the sticky dust in my mouth and throat. I felt like I could drink a whole lake without coming up for air.

Dad sat in the front with the driver while Tim and I lay on two skinny little beds in the back. We both jumped when the driver turned on the siren as we pulled out onto the highway. Neither of us had ever ridden inside an ambulance before.

First, they stopped at a little clinic so a doctor could check us out. I couldn't believe how dirty we all looked under the bright lights—the only white parts that showed on us were the whites of our eyes. I kind of scraped at my front teeth with my fingernail, trying to rub off some of the grime. Then the doctor came to look at us.

He poked at us, taking our temperatures and feeling our wrists. When he got to Tim, though, he frowned.

"I've got no pulse here," he muttered to the nurse.

I jumped halfway up, looking over at Tim. He was lying on the table just staring up at the ceiling, but I could see his chest moving. "Tim, are you OK?" I asked.

"Yeah," he said sleepily. "I'm just kinda tired."

That made me feel better, so I settled back again. The doctor finally found Tim's pulse by feeling the side of his neck.

By that time it was almost four o'clock in the morning. They loaded us back in the ambulance to take us to the nearest hospital, which was about an hour away.

Tim dozed off during the ride, but I couldn't sleep—there were still too many things going through my mind. It was like my brain couldn't catch up with everything that had happened in the last few hours.

I'm alive, I told myself. *I'm alive, I'm alive, I'm alive!* I'd gotten so used to the idea that I was going to die that it was hard to realize that now everything was going to be OK.

Once we got to the hospital they took us right into the emergency room. "Have you ever been hooked up to a heart monitor before?" a nurse asked me after I was settled on a table. "It's pretty interesting."

I took off my shirt and she taped some funny round stickers all over my chest, then hooked up long wires to each sticker. The wires were attached to a machine on the table next to me.

"Lie still, now," she said as she pushed a button on the machine.

For a second I wondered if I was going to feel a shock or something. But the only thing that happened was the machine started spitting out a long strip of paper with a bunch of squiggly lines on it.

The nurse ripped the paper off the machine and showed it to me. "See? That line is your heartbeat. And, let's see here," she smiled and winked at me, "according to this, it looks like you're alive and kicking."

"That's good," I said. I felt a little silly lying there with wires sticking out all over me. But when she started jerking the tapes off I wished she'd just left them on.

"Ow!" I yelped. "It feels like you're taking my skin off with the tape!"

She laughed. "If I took them off slowly you'd *really* feel it. It's always better to do it quick."

After that she rolled me into another room for x-rays, then a hospital guy came in with soapy water and a sponge. He washed my face and hands, scrubbing until the water in his bowl turned solid black.

"What have you been doing, rolling around in coal dust?" he teased. "It's going to take more than a sponge bath to get this stuff off."

"I don't care if I'm dirty," I told him. "I'm just enjoying being warm and in a room with lights."

A little later the doctor came in to talk to all of us. It ended up that Tim had a bad infection in his right heel, and that I had a partially collapsed lung. That was why I'd had so much trouble breathing there at the end.

"It's really not as bad as it sounds," the doctor told me. "If you rest it'll get better by itself."

Other than that, we were mainly just dehydrated. It was about 8 a.m. when they finally took us up to a regular hospital room.

At first they were going to put Tim and me in the children's section and put Dad across the hospital in the adult section. But Dad threw a fit.

"After all we've been through the last five days, my sons and I are staying together. Can't you put us in the same room?"

He ended up getting to stay in the children's wing of the hospital. "I'll be the biggest kid in here," he joked as the nurses rolled us in. I was glad he was going to get to stay with us.

I couldn't believe how good it felt to just lie there on a soft bed with clean sheets and warm blankets, and to watch Saturday morning cartoons on television. I'd almost forgotten what it was like to feel comfortable. The only bad thing was that they wouldn't bring us any food. Instead, the nurse kept making us drink some nasty-tasting stuff mixed with Coke. "We need to fill you up with fluids," she said. "Food can wait."

After she left I complained, "I bet she wouldn't say that if *she* hadn't eaten for five days."

"I bet you're right," Dad agreed. "I'd give anything right now for a big, juicy pizza with lots of sausage and pepperoni."

Somebody must have heard us talking about it, because that night for dinner they brought up a giant sausage and pepperoni pizza.

"All *right!*" Tim yelled. "Real food!"

We dug right in, and that pizza tasted better than anything I'd ever eaten in my life. But I was surprised when I got full after only two pieces. I could usually eat five or six without even trying.

"I guess our stomachs have shrunk," Dad said. "It might take a while to stretch them back out."

"Well, I'm going to start on it now," I said, reaching for another piece. If there was one thing I didn't need, it was to get any skinnier.

Dad and I ended up spending two days in the hospital, but Tim had to stay an extra day because of his foot. Pop and Grandma came to visit us every day.

"If you didn't want to come see us, you could've

just called," Grandma teased. "You didn't have to do something like this!" But she hugged us a lot, and you could tell how worried she'd been.

Some newspaper people also came to talk to us in the hospital. Tim and I didn't say much, but the next day Grandma brought us some of the newspapers that told all about us being found. It was strange to see our names printed in a paper like that.

"I guess we're famous!" Tim said.

Later on, *Reader's Digest* and *People* magazine called, too. *People* wanted to take some pictures of us in New Trout Cave, so Dad drove us back out there. None of us really wanted to go inside, but we went as far as the Big Room.

"We won't be ready to go back inside the Maze for a while," Dad told them. "I think we've all had about enough of caves for now."

By the time we got back home to Tampa, I half-way expected all my friends to be excited about what had happened. But when I told James all about it, he just shrugged.

"So?" he said. "Sounds pretty dumb to me." I guess he doesn't read *People* magazine or *Reader's Digest*.

It wasn't until a few weeks later that we finally figured out what had gone wrong with our lamps. We had used the same can of carbide that we'd opened the year before, and Dad thinks it might've gotten damp sitting out in our garage all that time, which made it not last as long as it should.

ONE YEAR LATER

"Next time," Dad said, "we'll take a fresh can of carbide, and we'll *each* carry a pack with lights and food and water."

Next time? I'm not so sure about that.

There are still times that I wake up in the middle of the night thinking I'm back there in New Trout Cave, sitting in the dark on a cold rock. My heart starts pounding and I feel like I can't breathe. I have to jump up and turn on the light to see that it's just a dream. Each time the light comes on and I see my room, usually messy, but *not* a dark cave, I'm so relieved I feel like yelling and hugging somebody. It's great to have a nightmare you can wake up from!

Then there are other times when I wonder if *this* is all a dream, like my broken remote control and Dad's Coke machine. What if I'm really still sitting in New Trout just dreaming that we were rescued? How do I know this is real? It gives me a funny feeling to think about that.

But more than anything else, I guess I feel lucky— lucky to be alive, lucky to still have my dad and brother. I don't know what I'd do without them.

I still think a lot about Mom, and how close we came to seeing her again. But I know now that it just wasn't time yet for us to go be with her. There must still be something else we're supposed to do right here.

And whatever it is, I guess it must be good!

Author's
Note

Several months after Buddy and his family were rescued from New Trout Cave, I visited them at their home in Tampa, Florida. I got to meet Miss Kitty and to see the red backpack that helped lead the rescuers to them. It still had black dust all over it.

I also got to visit New Trout Cave myself, with John Hempel and Martin Hardy as guides. The cave was just as Buddy had described it—dark and cold, and very dusty. I saw one little brown bat hanging on a wall, and was careful not to disturb it.

Then Mr. Hempel and Mr. Hardy led me back through the cave. We tried to follow the same path Buddy had taken—down the main tunnel, into the Big Room, then on into the Maze. I made sure to sign my name in the Big Room register, which was still lying on a rock there.

Once we started into the Maze, I noticed that Mr. Hardy was stopping at each turn to tear off strips of some bright pink tape and stick it onto the rocks, making tape "arrows" to point back the way we came.

"I don't usually do this," he told me, "but after what happened to the Luteses I'd rather not take any chances. We'll remove the tape on our way out."

Soon we reached the ledge where the Lutes' red backpack had been found and climbed down into the drop-off. It was a tight squeeze to get through into the next tunnel; so tight, in fact, that the battery pack I was wearing on my belt—I had a battery-powered headlamp, not a carbide one—got knocked off. My batteries went flying down somewhere onto the rocks, and my lamp went out.

Luckily, Mr. Hempel had brought along some extra batteries, so before long I had a light again. Just those few moments in the dark were more than enough for me.

Eventually we found the room where Buddy and his family had waited for so long. I climbed up on the big boulder and sat, as Buddy had, with my knees up to my chest. Even with our three small lights shining, the room wasn't at all comfortable. I was glad when we started out again.

Back outside, I had to laugh when I looked at Mr. Hempel and Mr. Hardy—their faces and clothes were black with dust! But when I looked down at myself, I discovered I was just as dirty.

I learned a lot from Buddy about caves and

about the people who explore them, and also about how easy it is to make a simple mistake and end up in trouble. Many people who've gotten lost in caves haven't survived to tell the story. It's a miracle that the Lutes family did!

Their experience reminds me of verses in Psalm 139:

"Where can I go from your Spirit? Where can I flee from your presence? If I go up to the heavens, you are there; if I make my bed in the depths, you are there. Even the darkness will not be dark to you; the night will shine like the day, for darkness is as light to you.

How precious to me are your thoughts, O God!... When I awake, I am still with you." (vv. 7-8, 12, 17-18, NIV).